Runnin' the Show

Basketball Leadership
for Coaches and Players

**What I've Learned about Basketball Leadership—
on the court, from the bench, and at practice**

Dick DeVenzio

www.pointguardcollege.com

Second Edition

Runnin' the Show: Basketball Leadership for Coaches and Players
Published by Bridgeway Books
PO Box 80107
Austin, Texas 78758

For more information about our books, please write to us, call
512.478.2028, or visit our website at www.bridgewaybooks.net.

Library of Congress Control Number: 2006925009

ISBN-13: 978-1-933538-53-2
ISBN-10: 1-933538-53-8

Original publication date: 1999

For information, purchases or permissions, go to:
http://www.pointguardcollege.com

10 9 8 7 6 5 4 3

To Clayton Hepler —

I am looking forward to getting to know you. I hope maybe you can use some of the ideas in this book someday. I expect you to be an outstanding leader, although I probably won't be on the planet long enough to see your best work.*

*Clayton is not yet two years old as of this writing.

Table of Contents

Section by Section Contents

Runnin' the Show

Runnin' the show" is a phrase used by a lot of people for a lot of things, but one of the most common uses has to be that of basketball coaches to indicate the importance of good leadership on a basketball court, usually by a point guard. A good point guard is supposed to be "a coach on the court." In this book, the phrase encompasses that meaning, but also includes good leadership by a coach, leadership in the off-season, leadership off the court, and some other ideas related to successfully leading a team.

It takes a great deal of intelligence, energy, and knowledge to run the show successfully on a basketball court, just as it does in a business, school or government. Leaders on and off the court have to sell their dreams, get a team to work together, initiate action, inspire athletes, judge talent, urge perseverance, and understand people, personalities, and motivation.

This book was written for basketball coaches, but it offers insights, tips and methods for anyone who would like to get a better grip on the many facets and opportunities of leadership.

88 X 44 Leadership

During summer sessions at the Point Guard College, I often choose one of the 4.0 students in attendance to answer a simple question that you would assume they would know:

What are the dimensions of a basketball court?

The dimensions can vary, but most of the courts in the nation at colleges and at city arenas where high school, college, and pro games may at different times be played have the same dimensions.

Usually I point out that nearly all football players, even those who have been hit in the head as much as a tackling dummy, will readily offer the correct answer to "How long is a football field?" Most everyone knows that a football field is 100 yards long, probably because of the simple, round number. In fact, a lot of people judge distances by how many football fields away they are, like a street or house or landmark. But rarely does anyone think in terms of how many basketball courts away something is.

Basketball courts are 94 feet by 50 feet. Ninety-four isn't exactly a number that jumps in your brain and sticks. (Football fields are 100 yards by 50 yards. Seems basketball courts ought to be 100 feet by 50 feet. Wonderful symmetry there, but the basketball folks won't comply.) To most people, the court is long enough. And to old guys with guts hanging over their belts, an 84-foot high school court is a welcome sight (or even better, a tiny YMCA gym that might only measure 74 or even 60 feet). Get the rebound on one end, take a dribble and toss up a shot at the other! That's the American Dream for many an old athlete trying to keep basketball as a carryover sport. But I've digressed.

I ask every athlete with whom I work to consider playing forever on basketball courts that measure 88 feet X 44 feet, or "88 X 44."

Sometimes the more involved or fantastic the story, the more permanent the memory, so I usually tell athletes that I have hired a farmer to come in and lay down a three-foot manure strip all the way around our basketball court. That means we will be taking three feet off both sides of the court (or six feet off the width of the court) and three feet off both ends (or six feet off the length). Six feet from 94 leaves 88 and six feet from 50 leaves 44. In other words, a basketball court of 88 X 44. These are dimensions that people can remember almost as well as 100 yards. These are double numbers with a simple ratio and a nice symmetry. They are also numbers with a purpose. That purpose is to remind athletes not to go near lines, and that in nearly every big game, a player—for no essential purpose—steps on a line inadvertently and gets a turnover that never needed to happen. Why make yourself vulnerable to losing big games via turnovers or errors? Why not arm yourself with habits that will force others to beat you instead of allowing yourself to be beaten by missteps and *uh-ohs*?

It is possible to commit yourself to playing basketball on courts with dimensions that differ slightly from the referees' or the rules books so that you never have to worry about making the careless mistakes that happen so often to others.

Cut down on careless errors, play intelligently and consistently, and make yourself difficult to beat. That's the idea behind 88 X 44, and I hope, in general, the common sense behind my way of teaching basketball, leadership, and life.

The point guard is the leader on a basketball court. He or she is the player who brings the ball down the court and initiates a play or an attempt to score. I was a point guard throughout my basketball-playing career, and now I make a living teaching point guards how to maximize their abilities on and off the court. To play the position well, to lead a team to a championship, you have to do it both on and off the court. If your teammates don't respect you off the court, you won't be as effective in influencing their actions on the court.

There is *so* much that goes into influencing actions on a basketball court. I guess that's why so many fanatics like me think of basketball as not just a game but a matter of life and death. Or at least life. Basketball is life. It's getting people to work harder, to work together, to think intelligently, to use common sense, to make plans, to carry out those plans, to overcome adversity, to—yes—sweat the small stuff, and to succeed long term by focusing consistently on the short term. Need I go on?

Despite the many highly-publicized examples to the contrary—athletes spitting on umpires and fighting with fans, opponents, and coaches—athletics offer incredible opportunities for personal development, character development, and group interaction.

When you're trying to get an athlete to lead a team to a championship, you aren't talking about spin dribbles and slam dunks. You talk about how to get the talented players to use their talent fully; how to get big egos to tone down; how to get lazy players to hustle; how to get selfish people to sacrifice for the good of the group; how to get careless people to pay attention to detail; how to get angry people to calm down; how to get distracted people to stay focused; how to get substitutes to feel important; how to turn disappointment into motivation; and how to learn from mistakes, capitalize on weaknesses, and maximize strengths.

For anyone who has ever played sports at a high level, this is all just stating the obvious. An intense sports experience is anything but a mere game. It is life at its most basic level. A struggle for survival. A quest for victory in something noble or special—a piece of greatness.

We've all seen grown men cry after losing a World Series or a Super Bowl, and we've seen the jubilant celebrations of grown men jumping around like preschool kids, giddy with excitement, feeling the thrill of victory, the sublime sense of hard-earned accomplishment.

I am always struck by the power of doubt that surfaces during those celebrations. Nearly every athlete says, "People said we couldn't do it, but here we are. We've done it."

Athletes often claim they don't care what people say, but they sure do remember all those naysayers when they have finally triumphed!

Every triumph in intense, competitive situations is very special—an overcoming of odds, a difficult journey—and coaches and athletes of any caliber strive to duplicate the approaches of other athletes who have won the Super Bowl or World Series or NBA Championship. What you do is the measure of you, just the way a professional's performance in the World Series is the measure of him. Should your approach be less intense because the game is less publicized? The answer is obvious. The best way to get to those high levels is to learn to treat the low levels with that life-or-death intensity. Every athlete knows that, or at least hears it over and over again.

The quest is to give it 100 percent—or 110, 200, 300, or 400 percent!

Let's stop right there. Sports, done right, are important. They can draw from an athlete every ounce of mental and physical power, yet that may still not be enough. Let's linger awhile on percentages and on the concept of "enough," and soon we'll take a step forward in understanding what it really means for a basketball player or coach to "run the show."

Working with more than a thousand athletes each summer, I am lucky to have what most people would consider the "cream of the crop." They are motivated athletes. Most are personally recommended by their coaches and considered "students of the game." Most of them are good students, many of them straight A. An additional advantage I have over, say, a typical high school teacher is that the athletes I work with have paid for the opportunity to learn what I have to teach. This is their sport, their love, the thing they work on—most of them—every day of their lives. Nearly all of them have very high aspirations. Realistic or not, the majority have their sights set on Division I basketball. Duke, North Carolina, Michigan, and UCLA tend to be their favorites, and many athletes aim beyond to the NBA or WNBA. They are eager to learn, stars of their teams, respected in their schools and communities. So common sense would tell you that these athletes would surely give 100 percent during the five days that I have them in the summer. Yet I would estimate most of them give about 38 percent—from my way of looking at the approach needed by a championship athlete.

Thirty-eight percent is the level of effort put forth by dedicated, "cream of the crop" student-athletes with high aspirations and a quick willingness to tell anyone who asks, "I give 110 percent every day, all the time."

Let's look at what it really takes to approach 100 percent, and let's look at what good leadership is all about. Let's examine some of the magical stuff that can surround that 88-by-44-foot slab of hardwood—provided a team has a coach or a player who understands the importance, the possibilities, and the potential of leadership. I hope you enjoy this journey the way I always enjoyed flowing up through traffic in the mid-court area, passing up big guys, weaving in and out, and coming to an on-a-dime jump stop at the free-throw line; looking and faking one way and then softly tossing the ball the other way as the only remaining defender goes flailing off; or grabbing air and feeling embarrassed about heading the wrong way, lucky just to get a glimpse of the ball as it is laid gently off the glass for a hoop.

Ah, you prefer a slam dunk at the end? Have it your way. I just hope I can help some of you "lovers" feel some extra passion and even learn something new about the incredible game that has taken up most of my life. Feel free to "jump around" as you read—like a coach who just got a bad call. The book won't mind!

— Dick DeVenzio

Foundations
Personal Experiences

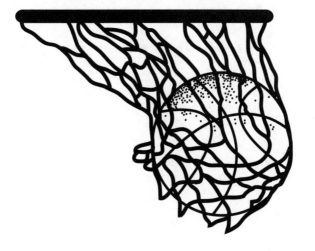

High School Success

Like a lot of coaches' sons, I could shoot pretty well by the time I was a sophomore in high school. I was 5'6" and 125 pounds—ready for the big time: varsity basketball. When that first varsity season began, I thought I knew my dad, the head coach. He had yelled and urged and criticized me every day on basketball courts for seven or eight years. But varsity basketball was different. These were real games. The bleachers filled with people, the band played during warm-ups, and a newspaper reported the action. This wasn't just my dad and I now. This was the real thing.

In the first few games, I ran around, did what my dad told me to do, and found myself averaging about 20 points per game. Then we met one of the traditional powerhouses of our area, and I learned about basketball and leadership.

The coach of this opponent didn't treat high school basketball like playing kids' games. His teams didn't build their winning reputation by being soft. Little towns surrounding Pittsburgh, Pennsylvania, took their blue collar heritage seriously. They were proud of hard work and toughness. They had no interest in some 5-foot-6-inch squirt sending them down to defeat. Before the game, the coach was in the locker room revving up his players, particularly one much-publicized senior football player, about 6'1" and 180 pounds. I'm guessing that this is what the coach might have said:

If you have any guts, you aren't going to let some little pipsqueak score on you. You get all over his rear end and make him understand what Ford City basketball is all about. I want him to hate playing against you, you understand?

The kid understood. He hit me during the opening tap and stood beside me, taunting me during every free throw and break in the action. His coach had told him to be physical with me; to rough me up and see what I was made of; to see how well I could shoot knowing that a fist was going to land in my stomach just after I released the ball.

On my first shot, I was knocked down. But the referee, probably watching the flight of the ball, didn't see anything. Or maybe he was part of the blue collar Pittsburgh thing himself. Maybe that was all part of the growing-up process. A little kid 5'6", 125, doesn't get to swagger like an athlete in Western Pennsylvania unless he can take it. So maybe the ref saw the flagrant foul and looked the other way. I'm not sure. I just know that, during the next break in the action, I went over to my dad and told him what was happening.

"Dad, he's hitting me," I said.

My dad's response (himself a successful coach with the Pittsburgh blue-collar pride and toughness) was instantaneous and thunderous.

"Darn right he's hitting you. I'm going to hit you double if you don't start moving your lazy *ass!* How can you be so dumb? Why the hell would you just stand there and let a guy hit you? Is that all the sense you have? You don't just stand there and let a bigger guy hit you. Don't you see Gary Reed over there? *Gawd darn,* how can you be so dumb! Gary's been beating up everyone in town for the last ten years, and you're over here telling me that some kid's hitting you. For *krissake,* take him over to Gary. Haven't you ever heard of a screen? Don't you know Gary's on your team? Do you think Gary's afraid of a little physical contact? For *krissake,* run him over Gary, run him off Gary, run him beside Gary, run him through Gary. If Gary's a wuss like you, then we can all go home."

Making Adjustments

To this day, when I hear TV commentators discuss at halftime the "adjustments" some coach is making in the locker room, it makes me laugh. Sure, every once in awhile there is some strategy or different technique that can be employed, but what mostly happens is a coach gets in your face and reminds you what sports are all about. It comes down a lot more to doin' things than to talkin' about 'em. Proud Pittsburghers would call it a simple matter of rolling up your sleeves, putting your body and soul on the line, and not complaining, whining, or looking for scapegoats, escape routes, or excuses. Nike calls it just doin' it.

When play resumed, I was a totally different player. I ran my defender over Gary, off Gary, beside Gary, and through Gary—the precise "adjustment" my coach had told me to make.

Gary loved every minute of it and didn't have to be let in on the plan. Gary was 6'4" and 280 pounds, and he could move. Gary was a classic '60s bully. After school, as a junior high kid, he liked to wrap his arms around high school kids who were walking down the hill toward home. Gary would hold them tight and listen to them beg to be let go. He loved the whole cycle, the initial calmness ("Okay, you've had your fun."), the threats ("You better let me go."), the panic ("Let me go!"), and finally the tears, the rage, and the surrender. Gary had great patience! He would put his 280 pounds on a kid and lie on him for half an hour, just for the joy of the human interaction! The sound and fury, the pleas and threats, screams and chokes didn't faze him.

Gary was an equal-opportunity bully. He picked on everyone, and he blew away the old notion that if you stand up to a bully, he'll leave you alone. Standing up to Gary only urged him on. He flat-out loved a tussle, and he loved having my defender always in his vicinity. Gary smacked the kid guarding me, with an elbow the first time I ran by him, and the kid never even saw it. The kid literally did not know what hit him. But soon he was to know well. Gary stepped on his feet and hit him in the stomach, in the face, in the ribs, in the neck. Gary did everything to that kid that that kid had been planning to do to me, but Gary was so much better at it, so much more experienced!

Before halftime, I had 18 points and was essentially untouched except for that opening punch and the punch after the first shot. Also before halftime, the kid asked his coach to come out. He had had enough. He had been run through a meat grinder, and I had learned a lesson. I am not an advocate of hitting or hurting anyone, but I learned that day that it is often possible to take action in cases where you initially feel like a victim. Oftentimes, you need to look at facts from a different angle before you can take appropriate action. Today I know that lesson by a different name, and the story, I suppose, is more refined.

The Rusty Sword

A soldier was complaining on the way to a battle as he watched his leader, mounted on a big white horse and carrying a gleaming sword and shield.

"I could fight, too, if I had a big horse and a shiny sword and shield. But look at what I have, nothing but this old rusty sword. What can I do with this?"

When the action of battle got heated, the soldier with the rusty sword threw it down, deserted his comrades, and ran away. What could he do with only a rusty old sword?

Just about that same time, the leader's horse was struck and killed beneath him, and the leader's sword and shield flew away. The leader found himself dazed, on the ground, and weaponless while his troops began to give ground and feel their morale sink low.

While scrambling to his feet and trying to stay alive, the leader saw a rusty sword on the ground. He grabbed it and swung it around, hacked his way through the advancing enemy and rekindled the spirit of his men. He spurred his troops on to a glorious victory with the very sword that the complaining coward had discarded as useless or inadequate.

My personal introduction to varsity basketball and the battle of the rusty sword bear similarities. Both involved the failure to see the possibilities—the failure being a blindness or ignorance caused by misplaced focus.

A leader must always look for possibilities and opportunities and never give in to complaining or worrying about conditions or circumstances. A leader's assumption must be that someone, somewhere, given the same circumstances, could prevail. Then always look for ways to turn things around, and never sink into self-pity or get discouraged.

My father was furious when I complained about being hit because the alternative was so obvious to him.

"You don't have to stand there and let yourself get hit," he had said.

But most people in the midst of some doldrums just don't have the habit of diligently searching for a way out. I can tell the rusty sword story at one of my basketball programs and still have athletes complaining about being fouled in the gym a half hour later.

"Run, move, don't let yourself get fouled!"

I can't emphasize enough that I view this lesson as the most important one I know about leadership, whether you are a player, a coach, a parent, or a fan; and whether you are trying to lead a sports team, some employees, or a group of individuals spread across the nation or planet.

Someone, somewhere, could probably take your exact same set of circumstances and work wonders. Certainly all the people around the world, hooked to respirators in hospitals and gasping for breath, would love the opportunity to give it a try. This kind of thought is never far from me. I think it ought to be with every would-be leader. You may not be able to do what you're trying to do, but it probably is do-able. So it makes sense to stop all complaining and learn to spend all of your time searching for solutions.

Good luck.

College Failure

Oftentimes the people who write books just happened to be lucky or specially gifted at doing something, and their success gives them the right or the opportunity to tell you how it's done.

I remember the gorgeous woman, best known as the wife of Jake LaMotta ("The Bull"), who was turned into a spokesperson for an amazing skin care product. Vickie LaMotta was fifty years old or more but looked like she was eighteen. Her skin was perfect, and she was the perfect person to help market a skin care product. The problem was, they forgot to teach her how to lie. On tour demonstrating the terrific new stuff that would help everyone have skin like hers, a reporter asked her: "How long have you used Amazing Skin?"

"Who me?" she answered. "I never put anything on my face!"

In the same way, Deion Sanders could write a book on how to cover wide receivers. He could offer you all sorts of technical details on how it's done. But the fact is, he could cover a man like a glove long before he could put the technical details of how he did that into words. He just stuck on his guy. No doubt it helped that he woke up one day and discovered he could run forty yards in less than four-and-a-half seconds. Sure, he probably worked on his speed, but he had gobs of it before he ever stepped onto a track.

You know what I'm talking about. Nothing against Deion. He's a great athlete. He just may not be the best person to teach you how to run fast or how to cover a pass, even though he is extremely good at both. I may not be the best person to talk to you about leadership on a basketball court either, but I sure have thought a lot about it and experienced it from a number of perspectives.

First, I played on a dream high school basketball team. My father and I moved into a town whose team usually finished last in its league, as it had done the year before we got there. Together, we transformed them. As the coach, my father knew the way, and I, as a player, helped to pave it.

I made a quick decision, before the start of that season, not to become the team's top scorer. I had averaged 31 points a game during my junior season, but my new team had a guy who had averaged 24. You could see a competition coming that couldn't possibly be good for the team. So the decision was easy. Anytime we got ahead and seemed to have the game in hand, I made sure he got the extra shots and I quit shooting. It was a good formula. We finished the season with an undefeated state championship. That team has been called the best team in the history of Pennsylvania. (I don't know if we could have beaten Wilt Chamberlain's team back when he played, but we were good.) My teammate, Dennis Wuycik, averaged about 27 points per game and went on to be a pro. I averaged about 22.

People like New Castle High School's respected coach Connie Palumbo was once quoted in a newspaper in response to a question about what made our team so good.

"It's that young DeVenzio," he said. "He has tremendous belief in himself and it rubs off onto the others."

I appreciated the flattery and I think, looking back, that he was right.

I had learned a lot playing my sophomore year with Gary Reed, constantly calling on him to utilize his toughness to the fullest. I had learned how to use my own ability pretty well too.

People called me an outstanding leader before I graduated from high school, and I was named by *Parade* Magazine as the best point guard in the nation. I was on top of the world and headed to one of the best universities in the nation, athletically and academically. I chose Duke University after having Bob Cousy, as well as John Wooden, Chuck Daly, Dean Smith, and many other coaches make recruiting visits to my house.

I was one of those "can't miss" prospects. I could do it all—had *done* it all—had played in a state championship game against an undefeated opponent and had walloped them by 30 points before halftime!

There was no stopping me. I waded through my freshman year practicing and getting ready (freshmen weren't allowed to play on the varsity back then) and I spent much of the summer before my sophomore year playing one-on-one in Chapel Hill with pro stars Larry Brown and Doug Moe.

During the third game of the season, at Madison Square Garden in New York, the scene synonymous with truly great sports contests, I found myself leading my team—runnin' the show—as the clock wound down in a victory over Princeton. Bill Bradley, then a star for the Knicks (future senator and Princeton alumnus), watched in the stands with special interest while waiting for his team's practice to begin after our game. No one in The Garden that day could have missed the little kid in control of the game. I dribbled the ball, darted this way and that, and waited for a second player to get near me (one defender couldn't handle me alone that day). Then I passed to a teammate, ran and got the ball back, and started over again until I darted to the basket and dropped a soft bounce pass to a teammate for an easy lay-up. Basketball could be so easy.

After the game, our assistant coaches Chuck Daly and Hubie Brown (now basketball legends) talked to recruits like Richie O'Connor. They had to admit that this was my team and most likely would remain so for the next three years. I was a sophomore in only my third varsity game, runnin' the show at the point, controlling the action, doing it all, just the way the coaches diagrammed it on the blackboard. My college career seemed to be a laser copy of my incredibly successful high school career. What could go wrong? Princeton had a good team with John Hummer and Jeff Petrie. These were big basketball names, but they fell easily.

That first season had its ups and downs along the way. But everything pointed to the Atlantic Coast Conference Tournament at season's end, the big three-games-in-three-nights show of mettle that determined who got to enter the NCAA Tournament. There were no selection shows and at-large bids back then. You win the tournament, you go on. You lose, you turn in your gear, wipe away your tears, and start preparing to get 'em next year.

Despite some disappointing losses during that season, things seemed to be going in the right direction at the right time. We were peaking just when a team was supposed to, finally meshing our senior stars with our sophomore stars. A few games before the end of the season, we played a nationally ranked Davidson team in Charlotte. I had earned 28 points in a hard-fought overtime loss. A short time later, we played our final game of the regular season against our rival, the University of North Carolina. We played in Duke University's Cameron Indoor Stadium, home of the "Cameron Crazies." Duke vs. Carolina. The game. Then, just as it is now, the epitome of college basketball.

The morning of the game, I got a call from my head coach,

Vic Bubas. He was like a god, his office like a holy tabernacle. You didn't just walk in there, you talked to the secretary and she paged him on the intercom. (High tech back in the late '60s!) Bubas had been on the cover of *Life* magazine, the number one national magazine which rarely devoted time to sports. But Vic Bubas was bigger than life. He was a father figure. People talked about him running for governor. He was a thinker. He was more than a basketball coach. And he wanted to talk to me about something very important.

On the way to his office, it was necessary to pass through Cameron Indoor Stadium. Maintenance people would be in there, already spreading rubber mats at the sidelines, putting up folding chairs in the end zones, preparing for the excitement that was nearly palpable at 10:00 in the morning.

I walked into Coach Bubas's office, and he paid me the ultimate compliment. He told me he had been thinking about the game. (Really?) And he told me that he had a special feeling that he wanted to convey to me.

He said we had been through a lot, and he felt fully confident that I had made the complete transition to college basketball star. I wasn't a new kid anymore, so to speak. We had almost a whole season behind us. I was experienced and able. He said he was going to put the game in my hands.

"If you want to speed things up," he said, "speed them up. If you want to slow things down, slow them down. Just play the game the way you feel it. It's your game. I have complete confidence that you have the instincts to make the right things happen out there."

I walked out of Coach Bubas's office on Cloud *Eighteen*. Getting adjusted to almost any coach and coaching style usually takes some time. Should I do this? Am I supposed to shoot that? Should I pass more? What offense does he want?

By March, all my doubts were vanishing. In fact, all of *his* doubts had vanished completely, he said. The game was mine. Play it the way you feel it. Shoot thirty times or shoot ten. You decide. He told me I had his complete confidence. "If you get twenty turnovers, you'll only have your own embarrassment to deal with. I'm not taking you out of there. You are my man. You know how to win this game for us. I expect you to go out there and do it."

It takes a lot for a coach to have that kind of confidence in a player. And even more for him to risk letting the player know it. The game was in my hands, completely.

It was not an obvious decision. In our only previous meeting with Carolina, in January on their court in Chapel Hill, they handed us our butts on a platter. And as for runnin' the show, Carolina's coach, the now legendary Dean Smith, had unveiled his famous run-and-jump defense that day. This tactic forced me into making all the mistakes they expected me to make, just as though I were demonstrating at a clinic. I was picking up my dribble in the back court, leaping to pass with no one open, and then spinning around like a top trying to guard some "highlight film 2-on-I breaks" between All-America Charlie Scott and his counterpart, another 6'4" inch guard named Dick Grubar.

There was no stopping Carolina that day. They handled us in every phase of the game. Had we really progressed enough toward the end of the season to think we had a realistic chance to win the rematch? Did Coach Bubas know something I didn't? If so, I wanted him to tell me the secret. Had I really arrived, finally, as a college basketball star? He said I had. He said he had complete confidence in me. He said he knew that I knew how to win the game for us. I just hoped he was right.

Ah, the reverie. But, hey, let me get on with it and spare you the ancient details. We handed Carolina their butts right back. An eye for an eye, a butt for a butt—typical of that great rivalry. They beat us in Chapel Hill. We beat them in Cameron. I remember dribbling the ball around at the end of the game—there was no shot clock back then—killing time and gloating. They didn't have anyone who could come close to taking the ball from me. All those years of dribbling in my cellar, paying little kids to chase me around concrete courts, and teaching my dog a special dodge-and-dart game had finally paid off. I was playing in one of the biggest college basketball games in the country and the other team didn't have anyone who could guard me.

My coach had hardly given me any concrete instructions. He told me to just feel the game, and I felt it. I handled the ball, dished out 13 assists, scored 17 or 19 points, controlled the game, ran the show, and got carried off the court at the buzzer. What a way to end the season. I was indeed a college basketball star!

The ACC Tournament was just around the corner—no time to rest on laurels. In the opener we played Virginia and beat them handily. I think I had 22 points while runnin' the show almost flawlessly.

The next night we played South Carolina. They had Bobby Cremins and some soon-to-be NBA players: John Roche, Tom Owens, John Rikker, and Kevin Joyce. But I had arrived, too. Our coaches devised a defense that stumped their star, John Roche. I remember him being frustrated and just throwing the ball at the basket several times in the closing minutes. We notched game number two and I had played well again. Now only Carolina, whom we had just beaten, stood in the way of our entrance into the NCAA Tournament.

Going into the ACC Tournament final game, it would be fair to say I was in the prime of my sports life. If I played another good game, I would be named Tournament MVP and I would be leading us into the NCAA Tournament. It seemed to be inevitable: an undefeated state championship in high school, and now despite some rocky times along the way, the march to the national championship in college.

This time, Coach Bubas didn't have to say much to make me confident. I *was* confident. I remembered the game we had just played against Carolina at home. They had tried everything but nothing had worked. They didn't have anyone who really bothered me or who could keep me from doing what I wanted to do.

Carolina in the ACC Finals. No reason the game shouldn't be a repeat of the one we had just played and won handily. Three-fourths of the way into the game, it looked like a replay. As I recall, we had a 9- or 10-point lead at halftime, and we went up by 13 with about 13 minutes left. I was out there runnin' the show, feeling confident, smelling victory. I can still remember the looks on the faces of the Carolina players running up and down the court. They were doing their best to fight the battle, but they had given up. There was no shot clock, they had fallen behind, and they didn't have anyone who could keep me from doing what I wanted to do. I was runnin' the show, leading my team to a victory in the ACC Tournament final.

But may I digress?

Before that game, in the city of Charlotte, Coach Bubas had called me into his room, much like he had done before the Carolina game just a week or so before. Only this time the message was slightly different.

"Tonight, don't try to do everything yourself," he said. "Try to get David [Golden] more involved."

That was the essence of it, the next move of the grand master, orchestrating this championship. Only this time it had the opposite impact of the previous time. I am sure, looking back, that Coach Bubas's intention was to take some pressure off me. The physical and mental toll and pressure of having to win three games in three nights was well known and often talked about. Coach Bubas had to worry about fatigue. It was the end of the season, and I had played nearly 80 minutes in the past two nights and it looked clearly like another full 40 minutes would be required on this night. He must have thought that if he wanted me to have anything left down the stretch, he had to take some of the pressure off me along the way.

As is so typical in life, what is said and what is meant and what is understood can be three very different things. In a nutshell, I took Coach Bubas's message to mean that I was getting a bit too much publicity for a sophomore. I had been getting a lot of the press before the tournament had even started, and I was leading our team in scoring—while runnin' the show—going into the finals. Adding to that, the day before the tournament began, I was stupidly showing off for the photographers and got a lot of extra press. I really didn't think about it at the time. I wasn't accustomed to having cameras on the practice floor. It seemed foolish or somehow made me uneasy to have cameras aimed at me and to just be standing there, warming up and shooting around. So I stepped up my pace. I began dribbling two balls at a time all over the court, through my legs, behind my back, darting and faking, high and low. I really wasn't thinking of showing off. I just thought I ought to give them something to film if they were going to be aiming cameras at the court.

I was one of the few players in the country back then who could do that kind of stuff and, unlike Pete Maravich, I didn't get to do it in games. So, there I was showing off in practice. My teammates, of course, knew that I didn't usually do that stuff in practice. I was caught up in the attention.

It all came back to me when Coach Bubas told me to get our senior guard more involved. He didn't have to say it, but I had hogged all the publicity for myself. The cameras were on me. A lot of the stories about Duke had focused on me, and now I was leading the team in scoring going into the final game against the Carolina team I had just dominated a few days earlier.

Get David more involved. To me that meant: Quit hogging all the glory.

There would still be an NCAA Tournament to play, the really big show. So it wouldn't be wise to go into it with a lot of jealous teammates.

Get David more involved. Don't hog all the glory for yourself.

For three quarters of that final game, Coach Bubas's instruction hadn't mattered too much. I passed up a few shots, tried to get the ball to David a little more often, and we were leading by 13 when Carolina's Coach Smith called a timeout. He undoubtedly saw the looks on his team's faces the same way I did. They had given up. They had to try something else.

What Coach Smith came up with I had never seen before, though it seems so simple in retrospect: a one-man press. When we took the ball out of bounds, a Carolina defender face-guarded me. But no one else was guarded. In other words, our center looked to throw the ball to me, but I was closely guarded. David, our other guard on the other side, had no one within fifty feet of him.

Get David more involved.

My first instinct was to run and get the ball. I was the point guard. The ball usually came in bounds to me, and I dribbled it up the court and started an offense. But Carolina was making it difficult. Did it make sense for me to run to get the ball against a defender when our other guard was totally left alone?

Don't hog all the glory for yourself.

When I saw the one man press, I moved out of the way and pointed to our center to throw the ball to David. David caught the ball effortlessly and dribbled the ball up the court, no problem.

But David was an outside shooter, a "two-guard," not accustomed to setting up an offense or feeding our other players in positions where they liked to have the ball. But one-guards and two-guards weren't as carefully defined back then. Or at least the distinction didn't occur to me. Mostly one thing was on my mind each time as I stepped to the side, stayed out of the way, and pointed to our center to toss the ball in to David:

Get David more involved. Don't hog all the glory for yourself.

So David dribbled down the court and put the ball in play. He didn't kick the ball out of bounds, nor did our team get five straight turnovers. Things didn't happen that fast. But they started happening.

Carolina's Charlie Scott, one of the best players in the nation and a future NBA star, had 40 points that night and is credited with engineering one of the great comebacks in ACC Tournament history. But, I have to admit, his super game has always been tainted in my mind. Sure, he hit some big shots. But they never should have mattered. The game was there for the taking, in the palm of my hand, and all I had to do was want it, grasp it, run the show.

But I didn't run the show. I stood off to the side and watched. And pointed to the other guard.

Get David more involved. Don't hog all the glory for yourself.

Our players, talented but not creative on their own, had come to rely on me to penetrate and toss the ball to them where they could shoot or take advantage of a lunging, recovering defender. We had a very capable supporting cast who complemented me well, but I wasn't taking the lead, and penetrating and pitching wasn't David's game. So, gradually, it became obvious that nothing was happening. Meanwhile, Charlie Scott began to hit his shots.

Get David more involved. Don't hog all the glory for yourself.

The Carolina fans got back into the game. The momentum began to change. The look of defeat vanished from the faces of the Carolina players. Their star, Charlie Scott, was picking them off the mat again. And me? I was standing off to the side, pointing at our other guard. It always seemed selfish to run get the ball when I was being overplayed and my other teammates were always wide open.

Get David more involved. Don't hog all the glory for yourself.

To complete the tragic tale, sometime during the game, I realized that I had stood by and watched, failing to make things happen and forcing our players to do things they weren't accustomed to doing. A point guard should know those things, but I never thought of them. I was focused on not being selfish, while Charlie Scott went on his tear (terror!) and the fans and the Carolina players got energized. With the score tied, I realized I had to get involved again, but the tide had turned. I got off a shot or two, and maybe one or two for a teammate, but our shots fell off the rim. At that point, I was probably playing more with fear of losing than with the dominance I had felt for the first 25 or 30 minutes. I let that game slip from the palm of my hand.

At the end of the game, Coach Bubas went to me, put his arm on my shoulder and walked to the locker room with me.

"I'm sorry," he said. "I lost that game. If I just could have gotten you out for a short rest, the game was ours."

A short rest? I hadn't needed a rest. I was energized and excited by the crowd, the spectacle, and the opportunity to step onto the national collegiate sports stage. But . . .

Get David more involved. Don't hog all the glory for yourself.

I hadn't wanted to use my energy in the wrong way, so I had stood to the side and watched our lead trickle away. I had handed the reins completely to David (not what Coach had asked for) and, when I finally took them back, I had lost control and failed.

I didn't say anything to Coach Bubas. It didn't matter anymore.

We had lost. He had coached his final game. (He had told me that he was stepping down that morning during the get-David-more-involved meeting.) What was the use of saying anything about being or not being tired?

We had future NBA coach and commentator Hubie Brown on the bench that day, along with future Olympic Dream Team coach Chuck Daly, future NBA assistant coach Jack Schalow, and successful college coach Chuck Noe—a lot of basketball brains and expertise assembled along with Coach Bubas. None of them thought to ask me during the game if I was too tired to go and get the ball. They just sat there and assumed I was too tired, just like I just stood there and assumed I should stay to the side. None of it makes any sense, but it happened.

I think of my dad's style of coaching, the style I was most used to. If my dad had been on the bench that day (and I mean this with no disrespect at all to the others who were there) we would have won that game easily. My dad never considered fatigue. He would have grabbed my shirt and asked me (an inch from my face) if I was too much of a wuss to go get the ball and win the game.

I would've have said hell no, I'm not too much of a wuss, but I thought you wanted me to get David more involved. And he would've exploded! I can see it now, finally, with amusement.

"I did want you to get David more involved, but not now, for *krissake*. How dumb can you be? Now's the time to win the game!"

How dumb could I be? Very dumb.

I stood to the side and watched the ACC MVP trophy, the NCAA Tournament, and my college basketball career trickle away during the last ten minutes of that one game.

You pay a high price sometimes for being dumb. And that's what I did.

We got a new coach that day, and he found out all about the tournament. The game was there for the taking, in the palms of the hands of the little man, but he didn't have the guts to grasp it. He stood on the side and just let the other team have the glory. He didn't have what it took in the clutch. A real star has to want the ball when the game is on the line. I had always been that kind of player. But that day, I just kept thinking of doing exactly what the coach had told me. I got David more involved. I did half of it, but I had gone too far and there wasn't any glory to go around.

For the next year, the new coach wasn't going to be as dumb as I had been. He put in a whole new offense and built it around the big men. He added "no fast breaks and no penetrations." No use keeping the offense we had been using, the offense built around me. I had shown that I didn't have what it took when the big one was on the line.

He didn't know anything about getting David involved. He didn't have to. My dad wouldn't have known either. It would have been absolutely obvious to my dad—as a coach—what needed to be done, and he would have demanded it.

Strange though, my dad watched that game—as a fan—and the first thing he said to me after the game was over was almost identical to what Coach Bubas had said to me: "Too bad you were too tired to take control. You had that game in the palm of your hand."

I broke down when I heard that. But he couldn't hear through the sobs that I hadn't been tired. I had all the energy in the world, but I lacked the mental framework needed to seize the opportunity. This event has had a profound impact on my thinking about sports ever since.

You hear a lot about being able to accomplish the things you put your mind to, but a lot less about how easy it is to fail if your mind is put to the wrong thing.

As a coach and as a result of my personal experience, I have always tried to ask my top players before a big game: "Is there anything I have said or done that is keeping you from fully using your ability tonight?"

I don't know if it ever does any good, but I always hope to have players out there on the court feeling free to win the game if the opportunity presents itself.

I finished my career at Duke playing almost forty minutes a game during the final two years and even being chosen a first team Academic All-America in my senior year, but never again was I the hub of the team. I didn't really run the show, just played

25

robotically, doing what the coach asked, scoring five or six a game, shooting rarely, hardly ever penetrating or making anything happen. I brought the ball down the court, played as hard as I could, tossed the ball inside and got back on defense, the way I was told. One time, at the University of Michigan, I recall walking off the court at halftime and being told by Hubie Brown that I was playing a perfect game. The score was tied and I had done almost nothing against a guy who couldn't guard me at all.

But that was my new life as the guy who hadn't grasped the brass ring when he had his chance. During my final two years at Duke, I was turned into a quarterback who handed the ball off each time to the running backs and stood and watched the game. My days in the shotgun formation passing to five wide receivers were over. As I've said, you pay a high price for being dumb.

At least, my experiences have given me a lot of special insights into the nature of leadership on and off a basketball court. I will spare you the rest of the details of my personal experiences and go on to the insights I have gained. I hope you find some of them useful.

As a Coach
Suggestions for Coaches

Pavlovian Basketball

Basketball is a thinking game but, as a coach, one of your major responsibilities is to take as many situations as possible out of thought processes and turn them into quick reactions requiring no thought at all.

For example, when a player catches a basketball, you don't want him thinking what to do, as though there are a lot of options. There is only one option. Look immediately, every time, to the basket. If there's no shot and no one open, then some thinking can kick in. But not at first.

Same with rebounding. At some point a player has to decide whether or not to keep trying for a rebound, but not initially. The only acceptable reaction initially is for your big men to head to the basket immediately, every time.

Those words are key: immediately and every time. I think it makes sense for you to make a list of things that your players recognize as requiring instant reactions. This is what I call Pavlovian Basketball, because these things are as automatic as Dr. Pavlov's dogs salivating at the sound of a bell.

The length of your list will have a lot to do with the degree of success you enjoy as a coach. A lot of things in basketball need no discussion and no thought. They must simply be trained as reactions. Here are some of my personal "instant salivations:"

- In practice, when my players hear a whistle, they stop. When they hear two whistles, they come running. If they see me point to a line, they sprint to it.
- In scrimmages and in games, a shot by the other team means hands up. (All five players, every time. Why not? It

should remind them to start their block-out dance—hand up, seek someone to block out, make contact, go to the ball.)

- A shot by us brings immediate 3-2 movement for the rebound. (Explained in its own section.)
- A mistake means instant hustle.
- Frustration means pick up a teammate.
- Ball going out of bounds, run toward it.
- Teammate trapped. Surround him.
- Full court press. Get strong and precise.
- Loose ball? Grab it. Ball to chin, elbows out.
- We lose the ball, switch ends. (Don't let athletes stand there gazing as though something unusual has happened. It's amazing how many players do this.) The moment the other team gets the ball, fire a gun in practice, if you have to, to teach your players to react immediately.

This is by no means a complete list, but I think you get the idea. A good way to review the basics before a game is just to call out the situation and let your players call out the response. If they can do it verbally, it won't be long before they can do it physically on the court—especially if you reinforce these things on the court immediately and every time in practice.

The more consistent you are, the more consistent your team will be. Dr. Pavlov didn't *hope* his dogs salivated every time he rang a bell. He trained them *until* they salivated every time he rang a bell. The dogs' reactions were involuntary, automatic—just the way you want your team's to be.

How many times in the history of basketball has a coach corrected a player, only to hear the player say, "But Coach, I thought . . ."

The coach says, "Don't think." And maybe adds, "It's a bad habit."

Is it a bad habit for a player to think? Not in general, but it is a very bad habit to stand on a court thinking about what to do in a situation that happens a hundred times per game—like the need to switch ends— and needs no thought at all, just a quick reaction.

Make sure your players know the difference between things that need thought and things that need reactions. Maybe even more important, make sure *you* know the difference.

Coaching the "Line Game"

Coaches have different styles. There are many ways to accomplish the same goal. I do not presume to know the very best ways to coach. But I hope many coaches will find the following somewhat unusual approach to be useful.

Emphasize Execution, Not Conditioning

Going into any season, it is customary for many coaches to tell their teams, "We can't be sure we will be the most talented team, but we can be sure that we will be the best conditioned team."

Vince Lombardi, the famous former football coach of the Green Bay Packers, has influenced a lot of people in the sports world with his well-known line:

Fatigue makes cowards of us all.

Aware of this truth, many coaches are determined to have well-conditioned teams that will be tough under pressure. Therefore, they go on to tell their teams how hard they are going to have to work—"harder than you've ever worked before!"—and how they need to be prepared physically to pay the price of champions.

Initially this sounds good, and probably tens of thousands of coaches use this approach to begin a season. Personally, I disagree with it. I don't think this approach is bad; I just think a different approach is better.

Make Laziness Work for You

Begin with the notion that just about all human beings on this planet—star athletes included—are lazy. Naturally, there are superstars like Jerry Rice of the San Francisco 49ers who became famous for his demanding workout routines; and there may be millions of athletes who overcome laziness and learn to get their bodies in terrific shape. But the basic fact remains: people are lazy. Therefore, I think it makes sense to appeal to an athlete's laziness in a special way and, in the process, to ignite his competitive juices as well as his aspirations.

In a nutshell, I believe in scrimmaging during each practice and in approaching your athletes in this way as you begin the scrimmaging/teaching process:

"This season, I am not concerned about having the best-conditioned team in our league. We are a basketball team, not a cross-country team. I don't think it really matters whether or not we can outrun them. We aren't racing them, we are playing basketball games with them, and we want to finish the games with more points than they get. As a result, I am not so concerned with how well you can run as I am with how well you can execute, how well you can do the things we need to do to score baskets and stop them from scoring baskets."

Of course, I know that being in shape and running well is an important part of basketball, but I want the team to know that I have no interest in making them suffer just to show that I am a good basketball coach. I am interested in them playing terrific basketball. Period. My emphasis is entirely on terrific basketball. As a result, my teams will not run sprints after practice.

Many of the teams I played on saved energy throughout the practice, knowing we would need that energy at the end for the demanding "gut checks" that we experienced during final sprints "to see who really wants it."

As a coach, I want that energy used throughout the practice on things I think are most important. Plus, I don't want any of my players' mental energy used on thinking about sprints. I want all of their energy focused on performance. So my practices—and each drill or game we play—all have this sort of introduction:

"We will do this next thing seeking perfect execution. Each time you do it wrong, you will hear a special whistle. When you hear that sound, I expect all of you to sprint to the line (at one end of the court) to find out what was wrong."

The Easy Way Out

What if they jog slowly to the line?

They can expect to run a sprint before I even begin to talk about the error.

Your players must learn immediately and for always that the easy way out, the lazy athlete's best course, is to make no mistakes or, if a mistake does occur, to hustle promptly and fully.

If *any* player runs at less than full speed on the sprint, he must realize that he will run again, down to the other end of the court and back. Players must understand that my intent is not to punish them, but to get them in the habit of hustling instantly and fully to make up for mistakes. They should also realize that basketball is a game of mistakes, that teams must constantly change ends of the court quickly and often (even when they are successful at their end) and so, as a basketball team aspiring to great success, we must have the ability—and habit—to change ends quickly whenever that is required or asked for.

Here, you cannot accept anything but true effort. When you blow your special whistle or make a gesture that says *get to the line,* they better show immediately that they are in a true hurry to get there.

Assuming they do hurry to get there, you give them a chance to get out of running any further. The idea is this: we are not trying to be a good track team; we are merely trying to execute perfectly the things that we are capable of doing.

Typically, a failure to execute results in a sprint to the line, a brief comment, and then an up-and-back (a sprint to the other end of the court and back). But here's their chance to get out of running. When they sprint to the line, I expect them all to wait in sprint-ready position (hands on knees is okay) while I ask what they think went wrong.

If they give me the right answer, we resume what we were doing by sprinting right back to the positions they were in when they heard the whistle. If they don't give the right answer, they hear "Go!" (merely pointing actually does the trick) and they sprint down and back.

When they get back, they hear my explanation of what went

wrong, and then they hurry back into the positions they were in when they heard the whistle. And we resume the activity.

Searching For Reasons, Not Excuses

The beauty of this approach to your team is that they become thinkers and "suggesters" and they learn to focus their attention fully on performance, not on excuses, as so many players do.

If they sprint to the line and they have the right answer, they avoid the down-and-back sprint and resume playing immediately. And that's really what you want, not the sprint. You have plenty of time to condition your players during a two-hour practice. As long as they are going hard doing whatever you are asking of them, they will get in fine shape for the games. But turning your team into basketball thinkers versus basketball excuse-makers is a whole different matter.

It's a thrill to experience—plus your team improves dramatically—the day you see your players hustle to the line and offer you no excuses about all sorts of things that went wrong.

"I didn't hustle, Coach."

"I didn't get my hand up on the shooter."

"I didn't yell switch."

You will hear wrong things that you didn't see yourself, and those things will often improve the next time without your vigilance.

As the process becomes familiar to your players—and it will happen immediately and consistently if you are consistent—they will offer their mistakes freely and make big efforts to eliminate those mistakes. They don't want to run extra. They will focus their energy just where you want it—on perfect execution of the things you consider most important.

Caveat. Warning!

Don't go pulling all sorts of wrong stuff out of a hat. I don't think you should surprise them with new stuff you happened to see. If you haven't talked about something, explained it carefully, made sure they all understood it clearly and you emphasized it repeatedly, I don't think you ought to include it in your "line game."

Intelligent, Every-time Reinforcement

You don't want your players getting the feeling you always manage to come up with something new that they did wrong. You want them thinking they can win; they can get out of running by doing things that are possible.

In other words, I don't think you can demand that they do forty-six things well, or else they get punished.

I think it is wise to begin with one or two things on offense and one or two things on defense, just a few things they can keep in mind and concentrate on executing perfectly—and just a few things *you* can keep in mind to see and correct *every* time.

On offense, you can expect that they will take only good shots. You can expect that they will take no unnecessary dribbles. You can expect that they will throw no errant passes. You can expect that they show only positive emotions on the court during play.

On defense you can expect them to get a hand in every shooter's face, you can expect them to block out and move toward the ball for rebounds, and you can expect them to move their feet on defense and avoid stupid reaching fouls.

In the early stages, it may be best for you to do only one at a time. Scrimmage and pay full attention only to shot selection on offense and seeing the ball on defense. When you are able, as a coach, to see those things every time—and to whistle and correct every failure—you are ready to add a point or two at each end.

Your consistency is crucial. If you notice a bad shot one time but then let bad shots fly unnoticed the next two times, your players will quickly recognize your inconsistency and the effectiveness of the line game will diminish. But if you are able to *consistently* correct what you consider most important, your players will quickly learn to do those things you consider most important, consistently.

Principles Requiring Consistent Performance or Punishment

As a good coach, I think you have to have control of the three major aspects of offense: shooting, passing, and dribbling. On defense, you have to make sure that your team is truly working to make it difficult for the other team to score, and you need players that have the right approach to playing and practicing the game. Those are the things I would build into my daily line game.

On offense, that means:
- LONHOBIRAT for shooting,
- P's for dribbling,
- Sure-Maybe for passing, and
- 3-2 movement for rebounds.

All of these requirements are explained in upcoming sections.

On defense, I expect to see:
- a hand in shooters' faces every time,
- everyone seeing the ball all the time,
- all five players in motion toward the basket when a shot goes up (I cannot notice every failure to block out), and
- a sense of urgency in each defender's body language.

That's all. I know we can't stop everything, but it has to be clear that we are trying very hard to stop everything, and we are not just standing around hoping the other team misses or makes bad choices.

As for attitude, that must be consistent. If a player ever makes a mistake and has a lapse of effort or obviously gives less than his best, for whatever reason, the team must be punished immediately.

Here's the end result of this kind of approach to your team: they will hustle and they will remind each other often of the things that you consider most important. They won't do it to be good citizens or good teammates or to be coach's pets. They will do it simply because they are lazy by nature and they will realize that reminding their teammates will save them effort.

If failure to go to the offensive boards will get them all a sprint, you'll be pleasantly surprised at how often your usually silent players will remind your lazy big man to get to the glass for a rebound.

So many coaches spend whole seasons urging their players to talk more—with little success, they will often admit. Their problem is that they haven't made talking an important enough issue. The line game, if you do it right, will take care of that for you.

You would do well to give each player, before practice, a sheet of paper with the day's line game requirements. And of course, the number of points on that paper could grow with time.

The first day's practice could have only one thing on offense and one on defense; and the players could enjoy an easy practice as they focused on those two things and avoided sprinting very often.

The first day of practice, as I recall, was always extremely difficult. Most of my coaches sent a message about how tough the coming season was going to be. I always wanted to send a message of how fun and easy the game could be if you just focused on doing the things that lead to success well and consistently. I don't have any problem with a first easy practice or with a whole week of easy practices, as long as you are building in your players the things needed to be successful as a team.

If your team can bring the ball down the court, pass it to each other, and keep moving until they get a very good shot—and then play hard defense at the other end and contest all of the other team's shots—your team will be just fine! You don't have to worry about being Mr. Tough Guy Conditioner.

Following is an explanation of the principles that I think are musts in coaching a successful team.

Attitude

I'm not sure if this one really needs an explanation. It seems like it doesn't, but then I watch games and practices all over the nation, at all levels, where the players demonstrate attitudes that I would absolutely not tolerate as a coach. It's not that I think I'm a superior coach, just that I think sometimes players' attitudes get away from a coach; a negative situation is allowed to slide and then it gets out of control. I think that, by including concrete attitude demonstrations in your line game requirements, you are much less likely to have to deal with negative attitudes on your team.

Any kind of negative emotion demonstrated on the court is a lapse that the team must suffer for. Shows of emotion (in particular, negative emotion) waste time and hurt team morale. A good team suffers by shows of negative emotion. So why have them? All on-the-court effort must be aimed at successful performance. Period. Even players with bad attitudes who show a lot of negative emotion (and yell at teammates) will understand this in an air-conditioned room. I would explain this principle right along with the importance of getting good shots and contesting all the opponents' shots. This way, it doesn't get personal. It's just common sense. A show of a negative emotion hurts the team; therefore, the team will suffer for it in practice every time it shows up.

Your "bad actor" may want to turn your whistle into a personality thing, but there's no reason to let him get away with it. You aren't asking him to be a great person or to think the way you think. You just don't want to waste time with garbage. You don't want bad shots, you don't want unnecessary dribbles. Why would you want unnecessary emotions that are not focused on performance?

If your players, as a team, suffer each day in practice for the lapses of one or two bad actors, the peer pressure is likely to change the behaviors for you, or at least alter them substantially.

It is important that you define the requirements of attitude carefully in an atmosphere devoid of challenge, hostility, or personality. It's a simple requirement of a team that wants to focus 100 percent on performance. It makes perfect sense in an air-conditioned room, and it will translate well onto the court if presented in this way.

Shot Selection

I invented the term LONHOBIRAT some time ago to indicate what I thought was most important about shot selection. It means, get a **L**ay-up **O**r a shot with **N**o **H**and up, **O**n **B**alance, **I**n your **R**ange with **A**dequate **T**ime to shoot.

The word covers most of what is important in selecting shots but, over a period of time, I found myself changing my own way of teaching shot selection. Yes, those are still the ingredients to be considered, but now I use a numbering system. I begin by simply watching a scrimmage and requiring that my players find a shot that elates me.

When they get a shot that elates me, I call it a 7. If we get a wide open lay-up—a shot we will literally make 99 times out of a hundred, I give that a 9. There is no such thing as a perfect 10. Even an NBA superstar with a wide open dunk can miss. So the best shot possible is a 9.

During a practice, when I call something as not a particularly good shot, a player is likely to argue, "Coach, I can make that shot."

Indeed, he may very well have just made it. But the problem is, too many shots that athletes choose in practice may score against the second team defense but not against the better players they will face in big games. In other words, the so-so shot that manages to go in during practice too often misses during a game. As a result, you look back after a big game that you lost by a few points and you have to admit that you chose your way to failure. The other team didn't beat you. You chose shots that were so-so and it's no big surprise that you missed them.

You cannot let your team choose the very shots in practice that will assure them of losing big games for you. Therefore, other than wanting my players to know that being on balance, being within their range, and having adequate time are all important, I want them—during the action of practice scrimmages—to realize that I'm not interested in arguing about details. I just want to be elated. If the shot was taken a bit off balance, a bit too fast, or a bit too far out, who cares which bit it is? I'm just not elated with that shot, and so taking that shot in practice is not leading us to the promised land.

I give these so-so shots that most teams toss up willingly everyday in practice a 5. They go in fairly often, but they don't lead to wins in big games, which is precisely what you practice for. (You can win easy games without practice.)

So here's my rating system:

9 = a very easy, uncontested lay-up
7 = a good shot; I'm elated with it
5 = a so-so shot; it works often—in practice
3 = a bad shot; a very low percentage shot that everyone realizes should not be taken—you just can't have these.

When watching practice, I can yell out instantly what a shot is worth. Anytime I'm not sure, I yell the number in between. Am I elated? Then 7. Not sure, but it's better than a so-so 5? Okay, I give the shot a 6.

When you start thinking about shots in this way, and get your team thinking about them in this way, it becomes a lot easier to get everyone on the same page about shot selection.

Should everyone be allowed to shoot an open shot? Of course *not*. Everyone should be allowed to shoot a shot that elates me. The more you practice and the better shooter a player becomes, the more I am likely to be elated by his choices. But every player has the same requirement: elate me.

The reason I have gotten away from talking much about LONHOBIRAT is the L part, the lay-up. I find one of the most common problems teams have is the number of lay-ups they choose and miss, particularly by post players inside.

You work hard teaching guards to look inside and get the ball inside to your big men, and then your big men toss up some whirling loopty-doo shots and—Hello? We're supposed to all be happy with them?

Sorry. Just because a shot is taken close to the basket does not mean it's a good shot. In fact, most big men have a habit of turning potential 7s and 9s into 5s and even 3s by tossing up shots that have very little chance of going in.

Often they are going to their weak side, tossing up shots over the hands of defenders who are taller, stronger, and better than the players they face in practice each day. Small wonder that they miss these shots.

Your big men have to be taught to go strong to the basket with their strong hand; otherwise, there is a very good chance they will take a shot that will go in only occasionally when it really matters.

Even more important, big men are very likely to shoot too fast, a problem most young coaches fail to recognize because they think the shot must be taken quickly to avoid nearby defenders. Yet the best big men in the world take their time and take the shot they want. They don't hurry. They rely on strength and technique, not speed and surprise.

You must make sure your big people take high percentage shots, just as you have to assure it in your guards who want to stand beyond the three-point arc and toss up prayers.

If you don't demand elation during your practices, you are very unlikely to find yourself elated after your games.

The best way I know to get the shots you want is by making them a requirement in your daily line game scrimmages. When you see a shot that fails to elate you, you don't need to bother with explanations that irritate your players. Blow that whistle. Get them to the line, and let some of your players say it.

"You weren't exactly elated with that shot, were you, Coach?"

No, you weren't elated. The shot went in. It wasn't terrible, but it wasn't great. It wasn't what you wanted your player to select. It was so-so, and you were glad the team recognized it. You could use a shot like that some day, at the end of a quarter or when a shot clock violation is about to occur. But you don't want your players choosing that shot in practice; and it makes things a lot easier to have some of them telling you, rather than you constantly having to correct and criticize them.

P-Dribbles

Unnecessary dribbles are devastating to a team, but many coaches don't realize this and hardly any players realize it. In my opinion, to have a good team, you absolutely have to control your team's dribbling. I call unnecessary dribbles "P-dribbles" because a pro player at one of my camps one day yelled at a little kid who was bouncing the ball at his feet.

"You are pissing away a valuable weapon," the pro told the kid. "Quit standing there pissing and go some place. Or don't dribble at all. You don't have to dribble if you're just going to stand there. You use a dribble to *go* someplace."

The kids that day started calling go-nowhere-dribbles *piss-dribbles;* and later—for political correctness, I guess—we changed the name to P-dribbles. The name is not nearly as important as the concept.

Most good ball handlers will laugh at a little kid who stands there and catches a ball and then bounces it for no reason before passing. However, most good ball handlers do the same thing themselves; it's just not quite as obvious to them.

Initially, when you decide to eliminate the waste from your team's habit of play, you will encounter resistance from your players who have the P-dribble habit.

"I had to get my balance."

"I was improving my passing angle."

"I was about to drive in."

You will hear all sorts of excuses if you try to eliminate the P-dribble yourself. But when you add the P-dribble as a line game no-no, your players will suddenly begin noticing each other's transgressions immediately. The excuses will vanish quickly and, again, you won't have to be the bad guy arguing over the relative merits of this and that stupid dribble.

I give athletes four compelling reasons for eliminating P-dribbles, any one of which ought to stop the habit. (But nothing stops it like the line game.)

Four Reasons for Eliminating P-dribbles

1. P-dribbles kill your explosiveness.

If you are in the habit of putting a ball at your feet, you are not in the habit of using one explosive dribble and you simply do not have the "great first step" that characterizes good offensive players.

2. P-dribbles slow down your team movement.

Even though most ball handlers will swear they can hit the open man off the dribble and see everyone cutting, no one does it as well off the dribble as when holding the ball in passing position and looking. Furthermore, even if you have a player who sees and hits the open man well off a dribble, not as many players get open because basketball players tend to stand and watch a dribbler and wait till he's done dribbling before making really hard cuts for the ball. Listen to all the claims you want, but know the reality: your team will move better when you stick a no-dribble rule into practice sessions. Just as they will move better when you enforce the no-unnecessary-dribbles rule.

If your players aren't going fast forward, there really isn't any reason for them to be dribbling. Yes, sometimes they may need a dribble to improve a passing angle or for some other reason that you may allow. But let me assure you of this: you will gain more than you will lose with a rule that never allows anything but fast forward dribbles. (I coached a pro team in Europe and had that rule.) Once you start allowing exceptions, you are opening up a can of counterproductive worms. If you decide that some exceptions are warranted, explain those exceptions carefully and then be a stickler about the rest.

3. P-dribbles hinder your leadership.

There are many times when the player with the ball needs to communicate instantly and effectively in order to make a play. However, if a player's habit is to drop the ball to the floor the moment he gets the ball, the opportunity for effective communication is greatly diminished. It is much easier to talk to teammates while holding a ball rather than while dribbling a ball. You can talk while dribbling, of course, but it isn't nearly as effective as talking while holding the ball.

Noise level in the gym and defensive pressure add more obstacles to effective communication. It doesn't make sense to reduce your effectiveness on your own.

4. P-dribbles often trigger traps.

Oftentimes, against pressure defenses, a dribble triggers a trap. If a player is in the habit of catching a ball and looking, he can set his teammates in just the position he wants when no pressure is yet being applied. However, the dribble habit often brings the defensive pressure before offensive players are in the proper positions to receive the ball. Once a player is dribbling and facing a double-team, it is nearly impossible to position teammates. At that point you just have to hope you find someone who has run into an open spot. You can no longer hope to place him where he needs to be when the trap comes.

It is difficult for your best players to learn good dribbling habits in practice. They are sufficiently explosive to have success in spite of not employing a great first step. Their teammates move well enough to get baskets against the second team. The practice floor is relatively quiet, so leadership and communication don't suffer excessively while dribbling. And the second team's traps rarely come by surprise, nor are they difficult to beat. Therefore, none of the four compelling reasons for eliminating the P-dribble habit is particularly important in practice. However, all four reasons are usually crucial in big games, in the playoffs, or when the opponents are as good as your team is. Your players really need good habits.

I wouldn't go overboard teaching my players the importance of the four rules. I would instead let them realize that, like all coaches, I have my idiosyncrasies and this dribble thing is one of them. It is also one of my line game, pet-peeve no-no's. That means to them, they don't have to bother worrying why. Their laziness and lack of motivation to do any extra running will be sufficient at first. They will notice each other's unnecessary dribbles and stop each other from doing them. In a short time, they will begin to see how unnecessary and harmful P-dribbles really are.

Sure and Maybe Passes

You have probably noticed that my first four crucial line-game points have nothing to do with defense. I disagree with coaches who claim that defense is the number one ingredient in winning games.

I have no doubt that the most important ingredients are offensive ones. You could have a terrific defense, but if you lose the ball before getting a shot, your opponent will often have the opportunity to score against no defenders on a fast break before your great defense has a chance to form. (Most teams can be stopped nearly half the time if you just manage to get all your players standing in the lane with their hands up. I'm all for defense, but you just can't pretend it's as important as offense.)

Good offense comes first. Getting a good shot will nearly always assure that you have time to get back on defense.

Bad shots ruin an offense. Unnecessary dribbles ruin an offense. The third thing that ruins an offense is bad passing, particularly "maybe" passes.

You cannot allow your players to throw maybe passes—passes that maybe will arrive and maybe they won't. Your players must care about their passing and learn to throw the ball to each other with certainty. They must throw sure passes, not maybe passes.

If you aren't sure you can get the ball to your teammate, hold the ball.

Take a jump ball if necessary. Take a turnover and learn to set screens and come to the ball. But don't throw the ball to the other team and let them get excited with fast break lay-ups. Throw the ball to each other, or don't throw it at all.

During your scrimmages, punish bad-pass turnovers uniquely. Traveling violations, three second violations, charges—these have none of the devastating effects of a pass to the other team. Your team must learn to pass the ball to each other. Pressure, full court presses, traps, double-teams, rotations—I don't care what defensive tactics are being used. Your team has to care about throwing the ball to each other and *not* throwing the ball up for grabs. A ball up for grabs that one of your starters manages to snare is no better than a bad shot that happens to go in. You have to punish maybe passes. Maybe they won't hurt you in practice, but the habit of throwing them is sure to hurt you in big games.

I think you get the idea. I am not going to list here all the things I would hope to require of my team during the course of a season. Most of them are listed in my book, *STUFF Good Players Should Know.*

I do think it makes sense to build your list one at a time, perhaps not so much for the players' sake as for your own. You need to make sure you will notice the errors that are on the list so that you don't miss many glaring examples. No one can see everything, but your punishments cannot become a matter of whimsy. Your players have to develop an expectation that they are unlikely to get away with a transgression of one of your crucial points. All of your players should be able to get good at doing—every single time—the things you think really matter.

3-2 Movement

There is no excuse for not having three players going to the offensive glass on every shot your team takes; and there is no excuse not to have two guards in position at the elbows of the free-throw line, simultaneously ready to get a long rebound and get back on defense.

To get this done, you merely have to require it in practice from day one. Start by demonstrating the movement when you are running through your offensive plays with no defense on the court.

Why is this so important?

Watch films of big games anywhere—pro and college included—and you will see that offensive rebounds are rarely grabbed by players who trick their opponents or manage by some special technique to get by a block out and get inside position. Instead, most offensive rebounds are grabbed by players who go to the boards and are not blocked out. Penetrations often free lanes to the basket, and sometimes defenders simply forget about blocking out. In any case, the important thing is to make sure your players develop the habit of always going to the hoop, never deciding if it makes sense in this or that particular situation. To be in position when opportunities arise, your players must have the habit of going every time.

In the same way, whether they are shooting jump shots, lay-ups, or "threes," two guards ought to get in motion on every shot and get to the elbows. If an opposing player is cherry picking, naturally one of your guards has to forget about the elbow and get back. But typically, five defenders will be in the lane, and your two guards ought to be leaning in to see if there's any garbage to pick up instead of watching the game near mid court and backing toward the defensive end.

Keep your guards near the action (it often makes outlet passes harder to throw, too) and make sure your three big men hit the glass and "go to a crouch" every time. If your big men don't get to a crouch, they aren't really in position to get a rebound.

Any time you don't see instant 3-2 movement by your players after a shot, your team ought to be punished. If you do it in practice as part of your line games, you will like the results during real games.

Note: Some coaches allow their players situational discretion. "If you shoot, you can follow your shot and someone else has to rotate back," they may say. I believe in discretion too in some cases, but it should be allowed rarely.

Where rebounding is concerned, I believe it's preferable over the course of time to have your best three rebounders always going to the glass (leaving no excuses) so they never have to think about whether or not they are in a good position. At times, your guards may be in good position for an offensive rebound too, but I would say, "Too bad. We realize we can't do everything perfectly every time. So occasionally a guard will cross a big man. Big deal. Let's make it simple and definite. Guards back, big men rebound. Every time."

Defensive Principles

Every coach has to make up his own pet peeves and points of emphasis. Here are a few defensive principles that I would put near the top of my list:

1. Keep the ball in sight at all times.
2. Contest every shot.
3. Never allow a right hand lay-up.
4. Do not allow the ball to beat a defender down the court. But if it does happen, there is only one acceptable response: a full, 100 percent sprint to catch up.

I would punish any transgressions of these rules on the first day of practice and every day thereafter; and I would add some rules about talking and switching and urgent body language soon after.

That's a good start. If I were you, I would just keep adding to the list, as long as you and your players can handle the additions. I would keep this warning in mind as I continued adding: it doesn't do any good to have an impressive list that your players follow well only half of the time. What you need is a list that they execute well *all* of the time, and then keep working on getting better and better at additional considerations. You may not want to end up with more than six or eight crucial points at each end of the floor. If you decide to add more than that, you better have some hawk-eyed assistants watching constantly for those additional points—and you better be sure you want their input and interruptions when you get them!

Assigning Duties to Players, Parents, and Assistant Coaches

One of the most important responsibilities of a good coach is to assign duties to the people around you so that important things get done automatically. I often wonder in amazement at pro and college football games as top teams get penalties for having too many men on the field. With all those coaches and all those players standing around, can't someone be assigned the job of making sure that twelve people never go out there?

For many coaches, the assistants are often more of a problem than an aid. The assistants don't want to be problems, but in their enthusiasm they may try to do too much; they may be talking when you are talking or they may bring up a point which they think is important but which to you may feel more like a waste of time or a distraction.

To make sure this doesn't happen very often, your assistants need to know when you want them to add something and when you want them to put their thoughts on paper and save them for a more opportune time. They also need to be told precisely what you would like them to be responsible for.

Rebounding stats, shot selection stats, minutes played, timeouts remaining—you decide. Give them things to do that can help your team improve. Don't let them sit around and be a problem when you can put them to work and help everyone.

The same goes for players on the bench. Why have them just sit there? Isn't there information you would like to know? Or that you would like everyone to know? How was the team's help-side awareness? How well did the team communicate? What reminders were offered by teammates? There is a lot of information that could be useful to know, and most teams have an abundance of people around who could gather that information. But no one asks them to do it.

Personally, I'm not very interested in knowing how many offensive rebounds we got unless I know how many were available. And I'm not nearly as interested in our opponent's shooting percentage as I am in knowing what percentage of the time we really made them work for what they got.

How many uncontested shots did we give them? How many fast-break baskets? How many right-hand lay-ups?

These statistics are rarely kept by the team stat man. Usually it takes a real insider to gather the kind of information that could be most helpful to you at halftime. You have plenty of insiders on your bench. Most coaches simply don't use these resources as well as they could.

Clipboards on the Bench

There is no reason why each of your players shouldn't have a clipboard on the bench, and on the sidelines during practice, recording the crucial successes and failures of the guy whose position he will be taking. A lot could be learned this way, both by the player keeping the stats and by the player being scrutinized.

On any team I coach, the player coming into the game doesn't toss a jacket onto the floor, he passes his clipboard to the player he is replacing; and that player continues immediately, recording our efforts to meet our objectives for the game on a play-by-play basis.

Busy, Not Troublesome, Parents

No coach is immune from meddlesome parents. I remember Duke Coach Mike Krzyzewski having to put up with the father of his center, Mike Gminski. Gminski's father took a year or two off work and moved to Durham, North Carolina, so he could watch his son. Sounds like a nice family thing, but it was a real pain in the butt for Coach K. The guy would sit back there behind the team and raise hell. Couldn't he have been given some kind of responsibility so he could feel a part of things and not be so disruptive?

I would have tried to put a camcorder in his hands and to ask him to keep his son squarely in the middle of the screen so that his son's performance could be evaluated perfectly. It would be useful for each player to have his own version of each game on film, and it would keep all the parents occupied, especially those who might otherwise be a problem for you. Not every team has parents with camcorders, but you get the idea. It makes sense to keep them busy in ways that can help your team.

I don't mean to imply that all players' parents are problems, but every coach has had those problems and, if hearsay has any validity, I would guess that parental problems are becoming more rather than less prevalent these days.

Utilizing the abilities of players, other coaches and parents during the games is one of the largely untapped areas available to most coaches. I'm not going to elaborate any further except to say that I think it is worth your time to sit down and carefully think about what information you could use or what tasks you would like to have done. Very often you could get most everything you want if you would take time to think about how to go about getting it.

A good coach needs to have a list of game and non-game stuff and who has responsibility for assuring that each aspect is handled.

Who will make sure a free-throw shooter gets blocked out aggressively, every time? Who will make sure the balls get in the rack? Who will carry the projector? Who will check on shoes, uniforms, and first-aid kit? Who will get the team warmed up? Who will count the lay-ups missed during warm-ups? Who will check on the team's grades, homework assignments, visits to teachers, class attendance? Who will invite new people to games? Who will make sure that some little kids get the thrill of playing at halftime? Who is in charge of post-game snacks? Who is going to write thank-you notes to the local press reporters and photographers?

If you are doing all of these things yourself or not getting them done at all, you are not delegating enough responsibility. These are other people's jobs, not yours. Your job is to see that a whole group of things gets done; there is not enough time to do them yourself.

Being a member of a high school or college basketball team should be a terrific experience for your athletes, not just a matter of attending practice each day and playing in occasional games.

Empower Your Leaders

I remember one of my college coaches saying to me, "You should have been captain of this team, but your teammates didn't vote for you." I felt bad at the time, as though I had done something wrong, until the day I heard Penn State football coach

Joe Paterno say, "College athletes, even at this level, don't always appreciate perfectionists. They don't necessarily want to follow the guys who push them to be national champions."

Paterno wasn't talking about me, but I like to think he understood better than my coach the problem I faced in college. My teammates didn't give me enough votes to make me captain because I *did* push them. (There may have been other reasons, too!) I recall specifically that most of our guys liked to play half court throughout the spring and fall because it was easier physically. They could shoot just about every time they got the ball, get off more shots, and enjoy playing. Of course, playing half court that way didn't help us improve as a team, but athletes often have conflicting ideas about what they want. So, absent a coach who would require or at least request full-court play in the off-season, we had a group of guys who played half court half-assed (the nicest way I can think to put it), and they resented my nagging about "running up and down like teams really trying to get somewhere."

I lost that battle in college, ruffled some feathers, and essentially gave up on that aspect of leadership. I have also learned something from it. I don't think it makes sense to have a team vote for a captain unless it is a secret ballot just to find out what the players are thinking. (As a coach, I would also tell the team that their votes would be viewed as recommendations—not for actually choosing the captain, but for my own information and insight.)

On my college team at Duke, the voting was a popularity contest. We chose a nice, quiet guy, a transfer student, who had never played a varsity game; he hadn't ruffled any feathers under pressure or caused any jealousy. He was nice to everyone and worked hard to fit in during his "sit-out" year. In fact, he turned out to be the only one among us who did fit in! The problem was, our team was leaderless for two years and very divided. Essentially, our captain remained a nice quiet guy but did little to lead the team. We were pre-season top ten picks for two straight years, but we failed miserably to reach our potential.

Hey, he can write his own book. Maybe he did deserve to be captain. Certainly, I'll admit that the problems on our team were hardly his fault alone. But my objective point is this: choose the player who can lead and who can get things done for you. Don't leave the position of captain to a popularity contest that your best leader may not win.

Once you have a captain, make sure you empower him or her. Give your captain real responsibility and let the team know that you expect their cooperation.

Give Your Players the Opportunity to Lead (Don't Dominate the Action at Every Minute)

I recall my father/coach yelling at me during practice, exasperated that our team had no leadership. No doubt, at times like that I had failed to tell someone something, because I can clearly remember him urging: "You gotta *tell* them. You can't just stand there and watch them mess up. Go get the ball. Tell them to give it to you."

I remember following an instruction like that with some particularly abrasive action. "Gimme the ball! Get outta the way."

I was straining and struggling to become a good player and trying to do what my father/coach wanted, but I often had trouble—amidst my stubbornness and limited experience—figuring out what it was he really wanted.

What I've learned since, while trying to see things from both a coach's and a player's perspective, is that a coach needs to give a player some opportunities to be a leader.

Undoubtedly, there were many times that I failed to recognize what a good leader should have done, but sometimes I remember doing nothing because my *very* vocal coach was right there, yelling every minute, telling us everything that needed to be done.

Under those circumstances, it would have been extremely presumptuous of me to tell anyone anything, The coach was there, he knew what he wanted; he had decades of experience, and he was proving every second that there was nothing preventing him from making known whatever he wanted.

"Oh, we need a leader badly on this team. Why didn't you tell him?" he asked me one time, with exasperation, after a teammate made some kind of mistake in practice.

I didn't answer. I had learned that it wasn't usually wise to say precisely what I was thinking to a coach. But I was thinking and would like to have said:

"I said nothing because you were there and you were saying everything. Why should I risk being wrong telling him something when I'm having enough trouble just trying to please you with my own play?"

My silence makes sense to me still. For a player to take the reins of leadership in practice, there have to be some times when the coach agrees not to say everything he sees, to observe silently, take notes, and then talk to the team—later—about what he saw.

When a player has the opportunity to play in games or scrimmages or practice situations, knowing that you aren't going to say anything, he is a lot more likely to use his voice to try to get the job done as well as possible. But if he believes you are going to interrupt and talk and correct constantly, he is wise to be silent and wait to hear what you have to say. Therefore, your constant talking is actually going to prevent him from becoming the leader you want him to be.

You need to give your players a realistic opportunity to demonstrate their leadership. Give them some leeway, some space. Make all the corrections and criticisms that you have to. Just hold them for a defined period of time now and then so your players have a chance to show you what they can do. You can't expect your players to take initiative if you are always taking it for them.

Define Leadership
(Let Your Players Know What You Want Done)

From time to time, I hear coaches say, "I wish I had a leader like that," referring to a player on another team as though leaders just grow on trees. Naturally, some players are more inclined to be leaders than others, but leadership is more learned than natural. A lot of what you get out of your players from a leadership standpoint has to do with how you well you mold them to be the kind of leaders you want.

Too many coaches sit back and wish they had a leader instead of helping to create one. Because leadership depends so much on knowledge and confidence, the most important thing you can do is give knowledge and confidence to your would-be leader. It is not especially difficult.

Take extra time to talk to your leader each day. Make sure he or she knows the things you want. Make sure he or she has information that the rest of the team does not have. That way, the team has to look to him or her for information.

Make sure your leader knows what you're looking for, what you think the team needs most, what upsets you, what delights you. Spell it out. Lay it out in black and white. It is very difficult for your leader to ever feel the crucial ingredient required of a good leader—confidence—if he is struggling to figure you out. Give him the benefit of privileged information. Make sure he understands you and what you want from him. You will make his job—helping you and the team—a lot easier.

Upset about Something?
(Maybe You Ain't Taught
It Well Enough)

One of the most important concepts for a coach to understand is the responsibility principle. If things aren't going well, you have just one person to blame: yourself. Somehow you just haven't communicated well enough or explained clearly enough or taught convincingly enough what it is that you want. I am thinking of coaches who are irritated periodically by players coming late to practice or tossing towels on the locker room floor or making too much noise on the team bus.

If something is important to you, spell it out. Write it down, and make sure your captain and your team understands fully that this thing is a requirement of yours.

Sometimes when I am running a program, I may begin to get irritated at a player for dribbling on the side of the court during a scrimmage. Many coaches may not be bothered by that, so the kid has no reason to suspect that it is annoying me. I start to get angry at the kid and then suddenly have to remind myself that the problem is mine, not his. During this program, I forgot to explain carefully and fully why I hate dribbling on the side of the court during a scrimmage.

Some coaches are apt to say, "If I had to stop to explain every little thing like that, I wouldn't have time to put in out-of-bounds plays, defenses, or offenses. Every day there is something new."

I don't buy it. Every day there is something new because you didn't take time to explain what you want. You think you are taking a shortcut by leaving out all the little things, and you find out the hard way that there aren't any shortcuts. You must attend to the things that matter to you, first and fully, and then get to the rest of the game as soon as you can. If your early meetings with players and parents are slow and plodding, so be it. Do what needs to be done. Don't go through a whole season being irritated by things you failed to explain. Stop what you're doing and explain. Attach consequences to failures and go on. There are no shortcuts. Every failure to please you is your own personal coaching failure. If you set things up properly, things are much more likely to go well for you. Good coaches enjoy coaching more than bad coaches, and it's not simply because they win more. They have learned to deal fully—and get compliance—with the things they require.

Good Coaches are Good Because . . .

. . . they realize they can't get things done themselves or by begging. You have to form a partnership with your top players.

When Chuck Daly was named to coach the Dream Team in Barcelona in the 1992 Olympics, he didn't suddenly begin ordering stars to do this and that. Although I don't know from personal experience what went on behind the scenes, I have reason to believe what I have heard. Chuck Daly was an assistant coach during two of the years I was at Duke, so I got to know him personally back then. What I have heard about his beginnings with the Dream Team match perfectly with what I know of him and with what I believe in. Daly's first move was to get a meeting with Larry Bird, Magic Johnson and Michael Jordan—his three top players. He asked them what kind of team they wanted the Dream Team to be. Did they even want a coach? Did they want to be told what to do? Did they want to practice and get in peak condition? Did they want to play together?

It would have made no sense to even begin trying to coach those guys if they didn't want to be coached. But once they gave their okay, said they wanted to be on a real team, to be coached, to get orders, to work hard, to receive discipline, and to do their best, the rest of the job was easy.

You can imagine Daly's first talk with the team. "Hey, you're all a bunch of superstars. You don't need me. I'm not fooling myself or trying to fool anyone else. You have to decide what you want this team to be. I have no sense of wanting to force my will on anyone. I have already talked with Larry and Magic and Michael and they said they want . . ."

You can imagine the impact. They want to be on a real team. They want to work hard. They want to be proud to be on the greatest team ever assembled. They want to represent the nation with pride and dignity. They want to practice diligently and play hard. They want to set an example for rest of the world. What do you guys want? How do you feel?

How is everyone going to feel once the three superstars have already decided things? It is hardly surprising that the rest of the team fell right in line, and the result was exactly what they talked about on day one: the best team ever assembled, the pride of the nation, an example to the rest of the world, and the most popular team in Olympic history.

Daly didn't make that team; he let them decide what they wanted to be and then he helped them become their own visions. I think every coach has that same opportunity, albeit on a lower level, to talk to the best players about what they want and then to work with them and the rest of the team to turn their dreams into reality.

Do you want to be a well-conditioned team? Do you want to be a team that is hard to score on? Do you want to be a team that gains the respect of fans, officials, and opposing teams? Do you want to be a special team or a collection of selfish individuals?

The way you develop a team has a lot to do with what you get the players to envision and agree to at the start of the season. It isn't that difficult to get a team to comply with your rules and methods if you initially get them to put their desires and dreams into words. That way, your actions can be interpreted as supportive as you help them get what they said they wanted. At times, they may need to be reminded that the way to their goals cannot be lined with tea-sipping and hammock-dozing. But that's what you will be doing, reminding them of their goals, not forcing yours down their throats.

The best coaches are nearly always the best at getting their players to take ownership of the efforts aimed at winning championships. The top college coaches recruit players who are very forthright about their desire to work hard, to win a national championship, and to play team basketball. Those goals may actually be secondary to the desire to make it to the NBA, but it is important to crystallize those goals when you have the chance.

It makes sense to get a high school superstar to put into words that he's willing to do whatever the coach asks to get the job done. Because once he says it, he is very likely to go along with things that otherwise might be unpleasant and cause him to balk.

Nearly every player will agree in advance that there will be tough times, temporary negatives, and some unpleasant experiences to be weathered. So get *your* players to agree to these, and remind them of their commitment when those unpleasantries arise. It's not wise to skip this part of your preparation for the season. It comes in very handy.

Talk to your best players. Make them an integral part of your processes. Get them to make sure your center goes to class, get them to make the lazy players hustle, get them to talk to the disgruntled players, get them to pick up the guys on the bench.

Coaching is a lot easier when your best players do the dirty work for you. Without their cooperation, the job is thankless and nearly impossible.

Few coaches involve their players sufficiently in the day-to-day operation of the team. The top coaches count this concept among their most valuable secrets.

Do Most of Your Coaching in Air-Conditioned Rooms

This may seem initially like a strange directive for basketball coaches, but it is advice I believe in strongly: Do most of your coaching in air-conditioned rooms. The basketball court is a place fraught with tension, anxiety, struggle, and competition. It is not the ideal place for learning or changing behavior.

When you have a special project player, a big lazy guy, a corner-cutter, an unwilling student, or a player resisting your style of coaching, you have to do most of your coaching in an air-conditioned room, outside the gym, away from the tension and strife. In an air-conditioned room, in a relaxed atmosphere, you have a lot better chance of carefully defining the problem and finding a workable solution. If you can't come to a workable solution in an air-conditioned room, there's really no use going on to the court. Might just as well give your guy the day off and come back to work on things tomorrow.

When you achieve a workable solution in the relaxing atmosphere, usually you make real progress in the gym. At least, when there are lapses of effort or respect or whatever, you have a basis for appropriate action. Until you have forged that air-conditioned room agreement, I can't see any purpose for letting that player into the gym.

Sculpt your art outside the gym. The gym is a place for unfolding, not creating.

Make sure all of your players understand the maturity equation. (I explain it in detail in my book, *Think Like a Champion*.) The difference between maturity and immaturity is one hour. Maturity equals one hour. A mature player doesn't argue with a coach in the gym. He performs, accepts criticism, does his best under the circumstances, waits an hour until after practice to express to you any ill feelings, misunderstandings, or disagreements that may have arisen during practice.

If you ever have a player who can't follow this equation, give him the day off and see him tomorrow—in an air-conditioned room.

Superior Practice Sessions

Nearly every coach in the world would admit that, given two teams of equal talent, if one of the teams practices diligently for three months and the other takes the time off, the team that practices will win easily when they meet. One practice here or there may not make any noticeable difference, but good practices over a period of time definitely make a team better.

This seems so obvious as to be unnecessary to say at all—except that many coaches seem very careless about their practices and, indeed, like players, many young coaches are more animated in games than in practice. The best coaches reverse this; they work a lot harder in practice than in games.

If you truly believe in the value of good practices, I think you have to consider carefully the following suggestions on practices, substitutions, and playing time.

You Need Winners and Losers— Successes and Failures—on Every Play in Practice

One of the biggest mistakes an inexperienced or ineffective coach makes is having practice after practice where it's not really clear if your players are getting better. Let me give a typical example.

Your team is scrimmaging. One of your players crosses mid court and dashes toward the basket, takes a so-so shot, and hits it. The defense grabs the ball, throws it back in play, and heads down to the other end, looking to answer that hoop with one of their own. All of your players seem to be enjoying the action—and their parents, if they are allowed in the gym, will undoubtedly be enjoying it too. Only you are unhappy. If you have been coaching any time at all, you realize that the defense wasn't particularly good on that last play. They let the dribbler get to the basket without even a pass or a screen. And no one seems to be too upset with the fact that he scored. It was a rather lucky shot, no reason for the defense to be too upset. The shot shouldn't have been taken at all, but the offense seems mostly pleased. They scored, and now they are running back on defense.

Why spoil all the fun?

The problem is, you know that the defense you just watched wasn't good enough to beat good teams, and the shot selection wasn't what it needed to be either. But you just watched silently, not sure whether to correct the defense or the offense.

This is precisely what cannot happen to you. On each play, your team has to feel a definite sense of success or failure, and it can't be based on the fact that a stronger, taller starter happens to hit a so-so shot over a weaker, smaller kid from the junior varsity.

Your drills have to be structured in such a way that people win and lose constantly. If the shorter, weaker player manages to get a hand in the bigger kid's face, that has to mean a bad shot—a failure for the shooter. The shot, even though it went in, doesn't count. Against the junior varsity, you are seeking easy, uncontested shots, not two points. Two points isn't good enough. You have to remind your players constantly to practice as though there are bigger, stronger stars in the gym, not the intimidatable second string. The things your players do on the court have to work against bigger, better players; otherwise the practice time is wasted. You are already, without practice, able to beat your second team. That is not the purpose of practice.

The purpose of practice is to improve. Therefore, success and failure have to be part of everything. Was the shot contested? Then chalk one up for the defense. Forget about whether or not the shot went in. That's unimportant.

In a dribbling drill, it can't be enough to zigzag over the mid court line. Was it bad dribbling or good defense, or vice-versa?

The players have to know. The instructions have to be more like: "Dribblers have to get from the free-throw line across mid court with no changes or just one change of direction. If you do that, you win due to inadequate defense! If you fail to do it, you lose due to good defense.

You will be surprised how quickly the effort and concentration of your players lags when there aren't clear-cut winners and losers in everything you do.

If you want your team to improve, you have to be creative in arranging drills and skill practices so that your players have the constant feedback of success and failure.

Play Ten or Twelve Players in Every Game

This advice seems unacceptable to many coaches at first, but I think most begin to be haunted after awhile by the logic behind it.

Most coaches have heard often—and have repeated often to their players—the dictate: "The way you practice is the way you will play in the game."

But what does this say to the players who never get to play in games? Does the converse apply? The way you play in games is the way you will practice? My experience with players who don't play in games is that they usually don't play as hard in practice. They don't have the same incentive; therefore, they don't do as well, and they don't provide maximum competition for the players who do play, so those players don't improve at the rate they could.

What's the solution? In my opinion, the solution is to play at least ten players in every game. Let them know in advance how much they are going to play, and let them earn additional playing time for good performance in practice and in the games.

"Performance" here, it is important to interject, does not mean scoring. It means usually rebounding, fighting for loose balls, defending, and hustling.

I think a good coach ought to be able to prepare the bench players to play without hurting the team. Watch any team scrimmage and it is seldom clear that one combination of five players works significantly better than three of those players along with two others. The nature of basketball is such that, often a team with too many scorers actually performs better when some of those shooters leave the lineup in favor of some hustlers who seldom shoot unless they have a wide open lay-up.

Every team is different and some will be able to use ten players more easily than others will. But over the course of a season, I don't think it is wise to rely on, say, only seven players. Besides the fact that throughout every practice you probably have three players not working to capacity to push the others, it also puts your team in grave danger in the event of injuries, flunk outs, or other problems that may cause you to lose a player or two.

If you have ten players playing in every game early in the season, they will work hard and improve throughout the season and will be much stronger players should they be needed in more prominent roles later in the season.

It isn't difficult to prepare a player to go into a game and not hurt you. Make it clear what your eighth, ninth and tenth players have to do to please you:

"Hustle hard, fight for loose balls, sprint up and down the court, keep moving and setting screens constantly, make a lot of body contact, don't try difficult things with the ball, go in and play error-free on offense, get the ball to the starters and hustle on defense and for rebounds. Recognize that you will probably just get a minute or two during each half, and that your playing time will increase as you show the ability to perform up to the level of the other players."

A minute here and there will add immensely to the players' confidence, as will the explicit order that you don't want them to go in there feeling as though they must prove something to you on offense.

Keep track of these extra players' plus/minus performance. What was the score when they entered the game? What was it when they left the game? How badly did they hurt you? Or did they help you?

If they hustle and are reasonably strong and athletic, there's no reason to fear any drop off at all, as long as you have some good players in there with them. It is almost impossible for an opponent to exploit intelligently your new, less able players in a short period of time. The added energy and incentive they have can often put their efforts for the team in the plus column even if they never score.

The absence of some of your team's scorers often gives comfort to your other scorers who suddenly realize that passing up a shot won't preclude them from still shooting on that particular possession. The ball is likely to get back to them. In other words, on many teams, playing the "extras" often leads to better shot selection.

Sometimes, of course, you can argue that, over a period of time, you must be hurt by not having your best players in the game. But rests are useful; renewal is useful; extra incentive is useful. A lot of factors promote the use of a full contingent of players in each game; but the added spirit, the team aspect, and the competition of your practices is number one, and it is probably the most overlooked by coaches.

Your subs just aren't strong enough? Keep them lifting weights during the season. Make them concentrate on the areas of the game that enable them to play stronger than they are.

I don't believe any coach who says he has no bench and can afford to play only five guys. I think he has to have more confidence in himself and he has to have a better understanding of how to teach athletes to perform.

Typically, the reason a coach doesn't have a bench he can go to in the second half is that he doesn't go to that bench in the first half. I think a coach ought to have pride in his ability to develop his bench in practice, and he ought to give them playing time in every half of every game, even if only for a minute each time. The effort pays off.

Note: If you have six or seven substitutes capable of playing at nearly the same level, I would use the sixth and seventh players in substitute roles during the last minute of, perhaps, the second and third quarters—and play them along with the best three or four players you can find. This will keep these extra substitutes motivated and keep them competing and pushing the others for playing time; and it will assure you that these players will be ready to join your ten-player rotation in case of an injury or in case one of them improves more during the season than a player who initially seemed a bit better.

Decide Your Players' Playing Time before Each Game Begins

The idea of setting each player's playing time before each game sounds crazy to those coaches who think they can make all sorts of terrific decisions on the spur of the moment. ("This guy is hot tonight; that guy plays better against zones; this guy moves better in the rain!")

I disagree. Few decisions at the moment are likely to be better than the decisions you make as you look ahead and plan for what you will face. More importantly, even if you occasionally make some better decisions during the game action, often the pressure of those situations will cause you to make much greater mistakes.

The mistakes I am talking about concern keeping your players motivated throughout the season. Few things are more frustrating to a player than having a good week in practice and then not getting into the game on Friday night—not necessarily because of being undeserving, but often simply because the coach forgot to insert him.

It's not hard to forget about a player on the bench, and it is extremely difficult to know at all times who could be most effective in what situations. If you're honest with yourself, you have to admit that, these kinds of decisions are often pure whimsy. You play your hunches, you hope they work.

I personally would not let so important a matter up to whimsy. I like all of my players to know how much playing time they have earned, and I like all of my players to know that the playing time they have earned is exactly the playing time they will get.

In a nutshell, I want the concept of a team effort to be real. I want our team to know that all of them—at least ten of them—are going to be counted on to improve each day in practice and to perform in each of our games.

On high school teams, playing four eight-minute quarters, I would let each pair of players (two players for each position) know how they will split the playing time, dividing the splits by quarter.

Some pairs may split 6-1, with six minutes going to the star and one minute going to the lesser player; while other pairs have 5-2 or 4-3 splits. Notice that the splits add up to seven minutes, not eight. That gives me the opportunity to use my whims during the last minute of each quarter if I want to, or to make sure that a player scheduled to play one minute gets his full minute of play should he not be able to enter the game immediately upon reporting to the scorer's table.

If you like this idea but are not completely sold, you may choose to use those 6-1, 5-2 and 4-3 splits only during the first three quarters and revert to whim during the entire fourth quarter—or simply play your best five players during that final period.

To make sure I don't have all five lesser players playing together at the same time, say, at the end of six minutes of play, I tell the players *before* the game when I want them to go in.

One pair may have a 3-1-3 split, meaning that the better player will play the first three minutes, his sub will go to the scorer's table at the three-minute mark, and the better player will report in again at the four-minute mark.

As you know, there is no guarantee that a player reporting in at the three-minute mark will actually get in at the three-minute mark. It may take thirty seconds or even a whole minute for a dead ball to allow him into the action. That's up to fate. Sometimes a kid slated to play for a minute gets to play two minutes. Sometimes he gets only fifteen seconds. It will probably even out in the end. I don't lament fate, and I don't expect my players to either. You take what comes and you make the best of it. Sometimes you get more than your share, sometimes less.

If a player reports to the table at the three-minute mark but doesn't get in until after the four-minute mark, the player leaving the game comes to the bench, gets a quick breather, and reports back in as soon as he feels ready. He may of course get in immediately or he may have to sit at the scorer's table a long time. I don't concern myself with the luck of the draw. In a game of inches, we can't be concerned with that sort of luck.

So, some players divide their seven minute sections as 3-1-3, while others could be 6-1 or 1-1-5. Clear? This last split means that the starter plays one minute, is replaced for a minute and then plays the last five minutes. I want to make sure, before the game, that I will always have some ball handlers in the game, always have some scorers in the game, and always have some rebounders in there. You get the idea.

These splits don't assure that you will always have your best shooters on the court against a zone or your best ball handlers in the game at the same time. But they do assure that your players practice hard, work continually to improve and to increase their playing time, and feel a desire to stay focused.

If one of my players is going to be disappointed with his playing time, I want him to know before the game. If he's not in the rotation at all, he needs to know why. If he's only getting one minute per quarter, he needs to know what he has to improve in order to get more time.

What I don't want my players to do is disappear and lose confidence. I want them to know that they are going to keep getting chances to perform and, the better they perform, the more playing time they will get.

In my opinion, the power I give up by surrendering control of substitutions for most of the game is more than made up for in team spirit, commitment, and confidence. This system says loudly and clearly to the team: I have confidence in you. Now go out there and perform. If you mess up, so be it. You have another chance coming soon. Get ready for it.

I do not believe in taking players out of a game for making mistakes. Does that make them less likely to make a mistake when they get back in? Or does it make them more tense and more likely to make a mistake?

During the course of the season, all players are going to make some mistakes. It is the coach's job to teach them in practice to take good shots, to play smart defense, to take good risks sometimes, and at other times to be extra careful. I don't want my players to have the added pressure of worrying if they are going to be yanked for an error, nor do I want them thinking that if they pull off some magic, maybe they will get to play longer.

I want them going in there and concentrating on executing at both ends of the court in the same way we try to do it each day in practice.

What about a Player Who is Hot?

Do the percentages favor sticking with a player who is hot? Experts in statistics tell us there is no such thing. A 50-percent shooter who has just hit three shots in a row is as likely to miss his fourth shot as he is to make it. There is no mathematical evidence that so-called hot streaks are anything but a statistical inevitability, just as when you flip coins. Sometimes heads will come up four times in a row, but not because that coin is a hot head!

Your best chance of beating the stat man is to have players consistently shooting shots they are good at. Then the streaks they manage to mount will just be a matter of percentages, not luck. The better shots you take, the more likely you are to make them.

Keeping a streaking hot player in the game is not crucial. What is important is that our whole team learns to play intelligent basketball, regardless of who is in the game.

What do you do about foul trouble, injuries, and other uncontrollable situations? You do your best! That means your eleventh man may have to become part of the rotation, or a "one-minute man" may get some time in another position too.

What if two players sharing the same position begin to perform extremely well and you want them both in at the same time? I would pair them, after the game, with different teammates so both would get more playing time and often be in the game together. But during a game, I am not going to let my whim change what I did my best to decide before the game. I have the last minutes of each quarter in which to experiment, and the fourth quarter too, if that is the agreement I have made with my team. That's enough.

If I tell a kid, "Hey, I would have played you but Johnny got hot," what do I tell him on the night I didn't play him though Johnny turned cold?

I want the playing time determined by overall performance in games and in practice. I have to believe that what is right overall will be more often right in the short term too. If Johnny's performance overall has earned him half the playing time, that's how much playing time he is going to get.

What about Blowouts?

You may gather from my recommendations that I am not a proponent of emptying the bench when our team is far ahead or behind. I have left the fourth quarter for impromptu substitutions, but how many players are available? Personally, I don't like trying to keep fifteen players happy on a basketball team. There just aren't enough minutes to spread fifteen ways.

If we are far ahead in the fourth quarter I may decide to use all of my one-minute men or the players with the lowest playing time; but this is not to make me appear to be a nice guy, and it's not for the purpose of going easy on the other team. I don't believe in going easy on the other team, nor do I ever want anyone going easy on me. That's point-shaving.

I think, to maintain the integrity of sport, both teams should try at all times to get as many points as they can.

I would play my one-minute men and least-playing players for only one reason—to get them extra practice so they will be even more effective during the next game. Remember, my subs aren't just along for the ride. They play in at least three quarters of each game, even in the very toughest games we have. They are expected to perform.

We don't waste practice time just because we have played well during the first part of practice, and we aren't going to waste the fourth quarter of a game just because we happen to have a big lead. We will use the fourth quarter to get the best practice we possibly can. If the competition is too weak to challenge our top players, then it could make sense to have the lesser players in there getting more opportunities and experience.

But, to be honest, I seldom see it that way. The competition is almost always challenging because we aren't interested in merely winning an easy game, we want to continue at every moment of every day—in practice and in games—to execute flawlessly. As a result, it is hard to imagine any five players on another team offering no challenge. We challenge ourselves daily, in shooting drills where there is no defense at all—and we still never shoot 100 percent.

We are always interested in trying to shoot 100 percent and in trying to stop the other team from completing even one successful pass. That's very challenging, so it shouldn't be surprising that I would be very likely to keep the same splits in the fourth quarter that we use in the first three. Our whole team needs practice constantly, and it's especially useful to have new people—not the same old guys (ourselves)—to practice against.

Spend 5 Percent Maximum Talking to Referees

(And 95 Percent Talking to Your Players)

I don't need to elaborate extensively on this one, but misuse of time is so prevalent that I can't help but add a few extra words. This is my pet peeve in basketball. I travel all over the nation watching high school and college basketball games and I am regularly appalled at how often coaches of teams playing poorly spend the majority of their time trying to help the referees do their job.

The misplaced focus of these coaches is truly laughable. They have a whole team full of players desperately in need of instruction, and the coaches are yelling about a touch foul or urging the refs to call a three-second violation on the other team's big man.

If you happen to have your priorities that far out of whack and you happen to be that stupid, don't show it. If you want to be a referee, then be a referee. But not when you are coaching. Spend your coaching time improving the performance of your players. Most of them need good instruction very badly.

Look at the title of this piece again. Bragging ain't a noble thing, but I am giving very good advice here—and few coaches around the nation are heeding it.

Throw Away the Handcuffs
(Let Your Players Do Their Thing)

You may not like to think of yourself as the town sheriff, but a coach can't help but be perceived often by players as "the guy with the handcuffs."

"If only Coach would let me just go out and play."

That sounds like a reasonable wish for a player. But, unfortunately, a group of players allowed to "just go out and play" rarely looks much like a good basketball team. They usually look like a group without a coach.

This lesson I learned long ago when our high school team, over Christmas break, would play alumni in practice games. The alumni would feature a collection of former stars and (some) current college basketball players that, on paper, would appear able to kill a group of high school players. But they never did.

One of their problems may have been having some out-of-shape subs, but their biggest problem was lack of organization. No plays. No timing. No group-understanding of roles. No one to keep them from just going out and playing. Translated, that means dribbling unnecessarily, missing open cutters, taking bad shots, and no sense of urgency to get all five players hurrying back on defense, every time. When players just go out and play, these errors and omissions are typical, and as a coach, you cannot allow them.

So, don't feel any guilt over the accusations that you restrict some of your players. Coach-less on the playground, almost all players play far below their potential.

"But Coach, I need to feel free to go out there and do my thing."

My answer to that would be, "But Player, I don't feel free with you out there doing your thing."

Necessarily, most of your players must be somewhat restricted in what they are allowed to do. But the way you explain this is important. The common parlance is "knowing your role," a phrase which I don't particularly like because every player would like to have a starring role. You want every player to want a starring

71

role. You want every player to strive to be a star. You don't want players to accept the idea of taking a lesser role. You want players to build stardom from the ground up, step by step.

In other words, I wouldn't tell a player that he has to know his role, so quit dribbling and shooting so much. Instead, I would try to lay out an opportunity that each player can feel free to seize. Take care of the ball, move quickly, make everything you do purposeful, and take a lot of shots. Just make sure they are shots you are good at.

The handcuffs, you may say, are still there, but the focus is different. Within these logical restraints, everyone is free to just go out and play. Until a player understands the difference between going out and playing his way and going out and playing intelligent team basketball, he will have a problem.

Make sure that your players—and their parents—realize that the problem is theirs, not yours. You want your players to feel free to do good things, and you want them to be reluctant to take foolish risks. The line isn't as fine as most parents and players think. The better the player, the easier it is to play with the "handcuffs," and the easier it is for you to encourage him to take initiative.

To get the best performance from your team, you do want your best players to do more than your worst players. But you don't have to emphasize the restrictions. Emphasize the possibilities instead. Turn in *your* badge, drop the sheriff thing, and give every player on your team the keys to open up their shackles. Tell them:

"Hey, just do your thing. Pass quickly, move fast, don't waste dribbles. Make everything you do purposeful and take gobs of shots. Feel free to toss it up there any old time you get the urge—as long as it's a shot that you make about seventy percent of the time."

If you explain things this way, your job should get a bit easier. Most players don't want to admit that "their thing" includes failing to hit the open man, moving slowly, dribbling unnecessarily, doing things without purpose and throwing up prayers at the hoop.

Most parents will be quick to agree.

In practice, with this approach, you are free to change your criticisms from "Don't do that!" to "Hey, that's not your thing, is it?"

I can picture a meeting now with some parents irate over the handcuffs you put on their son.

"Hey, I'm sorry. He misunderstood me. All I want him to do is go out there and do his thing."

Take Time to Teach Procedures

Inexperienced coaches are likely to shortchange procedural teaching, perhaps because they aren't sure how much procedures matter or they aren't sure what procedures are important. But be sure of this, whatever you fail to teach will be done poorly, so you better spend some time on procedures. You aren't going to build a winning team without them.

What are procedures? They are issues such as:

How do you want practice to be started? What do you want the players to be doing before you get to the gym? How do you want your players to huddle during timeouts? How do you want them to go into and out of games? How do you want them to be prepared for meetings? Are your players allowed to throw a towel, kick a bench, toss a paper cup on the floor, or treat the student manager with less than respect?

Leave procedures to chance or common sense and you are likely to waste a lot of time and to become irritated often.

How do you get your team's attention in practice? How do you want them to go from one drill to another?

Don't be afraid to bore your players with details or to put in writing exactly what you want. But only put in writing the things you really do want and plan to enforce. It doesn't do any good to have some impressive handouts about "bench comportment" if you or your assistants fail to correct transgressions. Same is true of warm-up drills. No use writing that you want everyone to concentrate on making each lay-up and then let your team go out there and toss up a bunch of experiments. If you write that you expect each lay-up to be made, then have a student manager, a junior varsity player, an assistant coach, or your team captain check for misses—and let *the team* run an extra mile on the weekend for each one. Your team will get careful without you ever having to beg.

In practice, I like to let one blow of the whistle mean "Everyone stand still where you are." Sometimes explanations are much more effective when the players remain very close to where they were when you saw the error you want to correct, and an "instant replay" is much easier to set up so everyone can learn on the spot.

I let two toots of the whistle mean "Everyone hurry toward me. I have something I want you all to hear." (And furthermore, hold all balls, don't shoot any extra shots.)

There is nothing magic about my particular style, but there is magic in having procedures that your team fully understands and adheres to rigorously. Good procedures save a lot of time, irritation, and misunderstanding. They are crucial to building a good team.

If it's February and you are still begging your players to put balls in a rack or pick cups off the floor—or if you are still doing those things yourself—you aren't spending enough time and attention on procedural details; and I have no doubt that your oversight is hurting you more than you realize in other areas that directly relate to winning and losing.

Consider putting your procedures on paper, one per sheet, and make sure they are absolutely clear to everyone. Then give out those sheets. Assign an assistant or a player the task of making sure that each procedure is followed and, if it isn't, that the transgression is reported to you immediately.

You will like the results and be able, from year to year, to turn them into "hand-me-downs" passed from your seniors to incoming players; you don't even have to think about them or re-teach them.

If you're smart enough to keep writing things down, handing them out, and assigning them well (including a procedure for transferring responsibility), you will one day very likely be an outstanding coach and you will hardly even know how you're doing it! (Most young coaches are very aware of how they are doing everything, because they are trying to do too much themselves.)

One Bad Apple

Most everyone is familiar with the phrase, *one bad apple can spoil the whole bunch*. This phrase has special meaning for coaches. But the apple is usually renamed a cancer. Get one cancer on your team and he can—and often does—infect the whole team. But the phrase says one bad apple *can* . . . It does not say that one bad apple will necessarily be able to spoil the whole bunch.

So, how do you prevent it? What do you do about it? The answer is easy if the player is bad enough. You cut him from the team, even if he is a very good player, and you live with the results. Temporary inconvenience, permanent improvement.

But often the situation isn't so simple. The "cancer" is really more of a headache or a pain in the butt, so you can't make as good a case for removal. You may not even feel that you *should* cut him, but he's a daily hindrance to happy coaching. What do you do?

The Reverend Martin Luther King, Jr., in his famous letter to fellow clergymen from the Birmingham Jail in 1963, said that his people could understand and endure the hatred of their enemies, but what was most exasperating was the silence and inaction of their supporters.

In this statement, in my opinion, lies the solution to a lot of coaching problems. You must mobilize the silent or passive members of the team, the athletes whom you think would be a joy to coach without the cancer.

It is very important as a coach to teach your good people how they can help you. Often, you have to remind them to stand in opposition to the cancer, and you have to show them how. If the cancer is talking when you are talking, they—not you—have to tell him to shut up. If he is bouncing a ball when he ought to be watching attentively, your players—not you—have to tell him to pick up the ball or they have to grab it from him.

Good coaches constantly remind athletes that winning attitudes and winning ways have to come from them. If it's always you doing the correcting, it begins to seem like you against the world. One thing here, another thing there. After awhile, even the players with good intentions get lumped in with the cancer. They are all distractions keeping your team from excellence—and you find yourself in a permanent sour mood.

To enjoy coaching, and to lift your team to higher levels, you can't keep correcting all the minor problems yourself. Your good players have to understand Dr. King's exasperation and yours, and they have to do something about it.

They have to be noisy in support of what you and the team are trying to do. To get that done, I think you have to demand their help and keep reminding them of all the ways they are failing.

If they are with you, they have to show it forcefully. If they are unwilling to help, then you have more than one cancer to deal with and your problem isn't as isolated as you thought. You have a *team* problem, not just one cancer; so, perhaps you had better redefine your procedures or quit coaching and look for other work.

I don't mean that to be facetious. Coaching isn't fun when a team's effort is spotty and their focus is distracted. A good coach has to create an atmosphere of excellence. You need everyone pulling together. You can't do it alone.

Define the areas where you need help and keep demanding it. When "the headache" appears, don't bother correcting him if you've come to the point that you feel you are no longer reaching him. Correct the players who failed to help you deal with him.

Let your players fight it out among themselves and let them decide what kind of team they want to have. Explain the headache to them and tell them what they can do to help. Either they are with you or against you. You can't live with a cancer or a headache, along with the exasperating silence of the uninfected. If your healthy players don't help you attack the illness, you will soon get sick of coaching—and then everyone will suffer.

Over-Coaching

This last section for coaches could probably be a whole book, but I plan to give it just a couple of paragraphs and let you decide if this section applies to you.

I think just about all teams are over-coached. They have a lot of defenses, but not one which they do particularly well. They have several offenses but too often fail to take advantage of openings and mismatches. They have handfuls of out-of-bounds plays but seldom screen well or make sharp, well-timed cuts.

I don't think there's a grand formula for how many offenses, defenses, and special plays any team should have. But I do know that most teams spend too much time going over movements and not enough time improving their execution. I am often astonished watching TV and seeing big-name college teams look completely baffled trying to attack a common 2-3 zone.

In basketball, variety is not the spice of life. It doesn't do any good to present a lot of different defensive looks if your opponents can keep scoring on drives to the right. Make sure your team can play the game and do the crucial fundamentals; then enjoy adding variety and wrinkles.

As a Player

Suggestions for Players

Reminders for Players

Larry Doty was a professional football player. I have seen him at work as head basketball coach at Linfield College in McMinnville, Oregon, and I have also seen him coach his son's Little League and Babe Ruth League baseball teams and his daughters' elementary school soccer team. Football, basketball, baseball, soccer. There probably isn't anything this guy can't coach because he's a true coach. He understands coaching and the importance of getting athletes to play up to their potential.

Watch him at a Little League baseball game. Actually, you don't need to watch. Just listen . . . "Concentrate, concentrate, hit the glove!" he yells to the young pitcher. "Give him a target, get that glove up!" he yells to the catcher. "Could be you, could be you," he alerts the shortstop, reminding him that the ball could be coming his way. "Back up, back up," he motions to the left fielder. "Just one more out, and you'll get your chance," he tells the first baseman, preparing him to bat in the next inning and letting him know that everyone's counting on him.

Just a few seconds between pitches and the coach has spoken directly to the pitcher, the catcher, the shortstop, the left fielder, and the first baseman. When the inning is over, he's talking immediately about a rally, getting some runs, putting up a big inning, reminding his players about a past game when they scored five times in this same inning. "See the ball, watch the ball," he tells that first baseman who is first up. Then he's already walking over to the on-deck hitter, who isn't on deck yet and wouldn't have known he was up second except that he's being reminded while being handed a couple of bats. "Get ready," the coach tells him, "this is your day."

His attention suddenly shifts to the players milling around the bench. "Hey, let's give Shane some encouragement!" he barks out, as he seems to look several players in the eye, awaiting their involvement. Then he's back to the batter himself. "That's okay. Wait for your pitch." Later he's telling the kid he's a good two strike hitter, before reminding the kid in the on deck circle that he can hit this pitcher, it's his day.

On the soccer field, he shifts his attention from one little girl to another, reminding each that the ball may be headed her way, to get ready to run, to get ready for this and that.

At some point, the coach on the other team, standing on the same sideline in this youth league, yells over to Coach Doty, pretending to be in jest while trying to get Doty to shut up. "Hey, don't you have a volume control?"

The other coach is quiet and inexperienced and doesn't know enough about sports to anticipate the things he needs to yell to his players, but he's smart enough to realize that Doty's constant encouragement and reminding does get his team to be more alert and play better, so the coach wants Doty to be as quiet as he is.

Ah, Coach, please. Quit noticing what Doty's doing and do your own thing! But the coach keeps his attention on Doty while his team suffers from his distracted attention and his failures to alert them.

Have you ever watched how much impact a good coach can have on little kids in a youth league game? If not, go and watch a few, and then think about it. On nearly every play, a little kid will play noticeably better if the coach calls out his name and reminds him to run hard or to be ready or to stick his face into the action.

In big games among college and pro stars, it's not much different, except that players often have to do for other players what good coaches do for little kids in youth league games. In big games at higher levels the coach is usually too far away or the fans are too loud for the coach to be able to remind and alert players effectively from the bench. The most effective alerts and reminders in sports at higher levels have to come from "coaches on the court," players immersed in the action themselves, who can remind and influence the play of teammates on the spot.

If I had to choose the one most overlooked skill in sports, especially in sports at the pre-professional level, I would choose reminders. Common sense is convincing enough: if someone reminds you of something just before you need to do it, you are a lot more likely to remember to do it. If you are lucky enough to have a mother who reminds you to take your homework assignments to school each morning, you are very likely to arrive at school with your homework assignments. If you have a secretary who reminds you each time you have a meeting to attend, you are very likely to show up at each of your scheduled meetings.

As different as people are, it would be difficult to find anyone who would argue over the fact that timely reminders are very useful in a variety of circumstances. The secretary in my dentist's office always calls the day before an appointment to remind me to be there at the appointed time. And it works! Sometimes, especially when I haven't been to the dentist for six months, I would definitely forget the appointment; but the reminder refreshes my memory and I get there just as though I'm Mr. Conscientious-Never-Forgets.

What's the big deal? Hopefully, you have guessed it and are already going over in your own mind the ways in which reminders are useful in sports.

The player about to shoot a free throw needs to be reminded to follow through. If he isn't reminded, he will often forget—and he will miss wide open fifteen-footers that would otherwise go in. The defender on the free-throw lane closest to the free-throw shooter is typically supposed to step in front of the shooter and keep him from getting a rebound, should the ball bounce back after the shot. This is an easy block-out situation *if* the defender remembers to move aggressively into the lane. He will remember just about every time, as long as he is reminded every time. If he isn't reminded each time, unfortunately, he will forget from time to time; and every coach knows that those "time to times" will someday cause your team to lose a game that never needed to be lost.

Big tough guys, if not reminded constantly, will forget to put their bodies in position to get important rebounds. Fast runners often forget to sprint down the court for easy, fast-break baskets. Able defenders often fail to get their hands in shooters' faces and, consequently, allow easy shots that could have been contested—and missed.

Game after game, season after season, generation after generation, athletes fail to do the things they *can* do on basketball and volleyball courts; on baseball and football fields; on ice, in the sand, or on clay. You name it, athletes forget it and, as every experienced coach will quickly tell you, these "unexplainable lapses" will happen at the most inopportune times.

Why do unexplainable lapses seem to happen so often to some teams but not to others? The answer is usually easily explained. Some teams have "reminderers" and most teams don't.

How do you keep fellow athletes from forgetting the stuff that you thought sure they would remember? You have to get in the habit of reminding them over and over again. Good players, leaders, and those truly wanting to win championships and maximize their teams' potential have to get in the habit of reminding their teammates constantly.

I get exasperated with an experienced player criticizing a younger player for a failure. "Whose man was that?" "C'mon, man, block him out." Or "Don't let him shoot!"

The star may see himself as a competitor or a leader, telling the young guy what he should have done. But is he a leader and a competitor? I don't think so. Anyone, even the guy in the stands who never played a game, can say what should have been done after the play is completed. It's too late then. What wins games and leads a team is the ability to tell teammates the things that need to get done before they happen.

Many athletes know at least some of the things that need to happen during a game, but few are in the habit of offering timely reminders before those things occur. If you want to have a positive impact on your team and make a real difference in actual performance, you have to do better than tell your teammates what they should have done. You have to tell them that what they will need to do.

To make this particularly emphatic, I will make just one suggestion. After each game you play, win or lose, replay the game in your mind (or watch it on film if you have a game film available) and list all of your reminders, all of the things you said that had a chance to impact performance *before* the action happened. A good player should have many dozens over the course of a game, one or two or three per play. But most players, even some very talented players, won't have any at all.

When you make your lists, look them over carefully. Figure out why you aren't doing more or what you could add. Think of all the important things that happened, or failed to happen, and how you could have made an impact if you had it to do over. The effort will pay dividends and help you to offer more timely reminders next time.

That's one good thing about sports; the same things happen over and over. The reminders that were needed in yesterday's games are likely to be the same reminders you will need for tomorrow's game. So, the better you get at figuring out what you should have done yesterday, the better you will be at getting the important things done tomorrow.

As I said earlier, reminders are among the most overlooked skills in sports. They work. They help teams win. They help athletes perform better. But few athletes use them with any consistency. If you want to be a special leader on your team, you must become an adept reminderer. Start filling the air, in practice, with reminders for your teammates. Start out with things that are easy. "Run hard. Go hard. Good play. Get ready." It's not hard to get started, and it's such a valuable skill to acquire and use.

Miss America in the Huddle

Like nearly every coach, when I am talking to a team, I want all of the players to look me in the eye at all times. If I move while I am talking and, in the process, move out of a player's line of vision, I expect the player to move accordingly so he doesn't lose sight of my eyes. Some times, I move out of a player's vision on purpose, just to see how carefully he is listening. (If he fails to move to see my eyes, he can expect to be punished after practice.)

You could call this common courtesy—looking at a speaker who is talking—and you may think this is merely what anyone would do who was interested in what was being said. But few athletes think of "practice talk" in this way. This could be a result of the fact that most coaches are long-winded, so athletes selectively ignore them. But that explanation is too simple.

First, yes, coaches do tend to be long-winded and for good reason. Athletes very seldom get what the coach is saying the first, second, or even third time. Most athletes listen, or pretend to listen, and then go back to playing exactly as they were before the explanation was given. Second and most important, practices for most athletes (even very good, dedicated ones) are sessions to be endured, gotten through, or survived in order to play in games.

Nearly every athlete has to be systematically taught (meaning laboriously, over and over again) to understand that practices are where you improve and beat the competition and, therefore, everything said in practice must be viewed with great importance—even though many of those things may be initially uninteresting or repetitious. I like to ask a group of guys this question when I'm coaching:

"Would you stand in the back and pay limited attention if Miss America were suddenly here teaching this new play? Of course not. You would be in the first row, leaning inward, inching closer at every opportunity, 100 percent retina and optic nerve. However you would treat Miss America is the way you should learn to treat your coach. It isn't easy, and it most definitely is not natural. But if you are planning to be a real leader, to maximize your abilities and your team's potential, then that's your task: to learn to treat your coach the way you would treat Miss America. Don't just go through the motions, don't just endure practice. Make the most of it. Be all eyes and ears. Be in the front row at all times. Be on a mission. Listen to each phrase; turn it over in your mind. If the coach fails to explain things well, then figure out what is truly important and how you are going to re-explain that to your teammates to help them understand what needs to be done.

"Don't fool yourself. If you go through practices just trying to get through them and get by, your performance in games will fall very short of your potential. You probably know this. Most athletes who take the time to read a book like this probably pay pretty close attention to their coach. But the problem doesn't end here. Because if you are a basketball player or a participant in any team game, then it's not nearly enough to congratulate yourself for being an athlete that pays attention.

"Are you in the habit of making sure your teammates pay close attention the way you do? Most athletes have to answer a resounding *no* to this question. They don't do nearly enough to make things happen that they know are important to a *team's* success. On a test, they are smart enough to pass. They know these things are important. But on the court, in practice, they have to admit that mostly they just take care of themselves, that all sorts of behaviors go on that fall far short of *the way of a champion*, yet they let their teammates' behaviors go on every day and make no effort to correct them.

"What about you?

"A leader doesn't just give his coach his undivided attention; he tries to make sure, every day, every minute that his teammates do the same. That means, while listening and watching and nodding, he also finds a way to look around, to be alert and aware. He knows how to tap a teammate on the shoulder or on the back; he knows how to cut off a joke and how to discourage conversation so that the distractions that lead to failure for so many teams don't affect his team."

My experience working with thousands of dedicated athletes tells me that most of them never even think about having any impact on these very important, everyday occurrences that can make or unmake a championship team.

MJ in the Gym

How do you get yourself and your teammates to practice diligently every day? In my opinion, it takes a constant effort of imagination before you can begin transmitting this energy to your teammates.

For example, I often say two things to athletes while they are practicing. First, a simple question: *Are you practicing right now in proportion to your aspirations?*

Most athletes who are working out in the summer or practicing with their teams in the winter are aware that many other athletes are also working out at that same time. During any given summer day, there are literally hundreds of basketball camps going on, all claiming to make athletes better. During winter, tens of thousands of teams are at practice. There are literally thousands of drills, techniques, and lectures going on at any given moment. Hundreds of thousands of athletes are vying for several hundred spots on college teams.

This simple reminder often has a sobering effect on athletes apt to "fool around" instead of practicing to improve.

Sometimes a second reminder is even more powerful:

"Imagine ten minutes from now, shortly after we break from this huddle. You are back out there playing, and Michael Jordan strolls into the gym and looks around. Maybe he isn't even watching intently. He could be talking with a coach or Scottie Pippin, with a friend or acquaintance. How would you practice? Would you go through the motions in the same way? Would you stay so quiet, be so listless? Would you fail to touch lines or make sharp cuts? I doubt it. Most athletes, upon knowing that a star athlete was in the gym, would run faster, work harder, and be more animated than ever before. They would want to catch Jordan's eye and win his admiration, even if he weren't watching intently, even if he didn't stay long enough to find out anyone's name.

"If you would pick up your practice effort with Michael Jordan in the gym, then you better find a way to imagine Jordan in the gym every day to draw the best effort out of yourself. What sense does it make to impress Michael Jordan for a single moment during a distracted conversation? Better to impress everyone around you every day and improve your skills so that when your chance to make your dreams come true finally comes, you can do your best.

"If it helps you to raise your level of play by imagining Michael Jordan in the gym, then bring him in every day."

The Rich, Red-Hatted Lady

One of my favorite teaching tools is to ask athletes to close their eyes and imagine they are flipping channels on their TV late at night.

Listen for the excitable English accent of Robin Leach, the narrator on *Life Styles of the Rich and Famous.* (Leach always seems to be describing in detail a lushly carpeted yacht or a great room lighted by a chandelier with nine thousand light bulbs.) Into this imaginary world comes a billionairess, dressed in a $40,000 gown and a big red hat—so big it contains a bird's nest. Several hummingbirds are buzzing around her head. She doesn't just look the part, she lives it.

One of her habits is to walk around the streets of major cities and make bets and propositions with the locals. See her flip a coin, hold it on her wrist and make an offer to a homeless man. "If this is heads, you get this ten thousand dollar bill. But if this coin is tails, I get your sack and everything in it."

The guy contemplates for a few seconds. Everything he owns in the world is in that sack, but it's only worth a few dollars. He has to go for it—winning would be enough to get him off the streets!

Long story short, it's tails. The homeless man loses, and the woman takes the sack. She won it fair and square, but the moment she is out of sight, she tosses it in the nearest garbage can. End of story. TV off. Scene changed.

Imagine you and your teammates are in the gym, playing basketball. The other team scores and several of your team members yell, "Hey, let's stop 'em this time!"

"Yeah, let's stop 'em!" you yell back.

At that moment, a woman with a fabulous $40,000 dress and

a huge red hat with birds buzzing around walks into the gym, looks *you* in the eye, and she says, "I'll give you $10,000 if you stop 'em this time."

Not exactly a torment. She's offering you money to do what you were already urging your teammates to do for nothing. Just stop them this one time down the court.

So now what? How do you play? Is anything about your effort, body language, or noise level any different from before?

It's at this point in the imaginary scenario that a lot of athletes who claim to give 100 percent have to admit they could easily step up their efforts if ten grand were the incentive. All of a sudden their 100 percent claims start to sound a bit hollow even to themselves. They have to realize that they don't quite give the effort that they like to pretend that they give.

Do these mental tricks work? A lot of athletes tell me that they try to think of that woman walking into the gym with her $10,000 bill stretched out.

Michael Jordan, red-hatted bird woman, ten grand, take your pick. Use whatever mental tricks you need to excite your imagination, to propel you to making your best efforts. When you've done all you can to propel yourself, remember that you have to try to help your teammates do the same. That's what leadership is, finding the buttons that will push each of your teammates toward their best possible effort and performance.

Good luck.

The Six-to-One Ratio

Here's one of the most common concerns of athletes who aspire to be leaders: some or many of their teammates (or maybe just one or two selfish stars) don't like to receive any instructions. The common complaint is "I would like to lead, Coach, but my teammates don't want to hear what I have to say. They won't listen to me."

Few guess that this is usually an easily altered problem—if the leader is willing to pay the price. There's probably a good reason why their teammates don't like to hear what they have to say: they don't say enough good things!

Though I am hardly an expert on personal relationships, I have tried to teach this same principle to my girlfriend. "Say more good things and I'll be happy to listen to you."

In a team sport situation, as well as in personal relationships, leaders should plan on saying six good things for every correction or criticism. And they should make sure the six good things come first. In other words, imagine a machine that only gives out dollar bills. To get one, you have to put in four quarters. Each time you want *one*, you have to put in *four*. In relationships, four really isn't enough. You need six most of the time.

If you have already built up a certain animosity or negative relationship with some teammates, you probably have a serious deficit going against you. Most athletes are rather quiet and then suddenly speak up when something goes wrong and they are irritated. If this has happened to you, you may have said ten or twelve bad things already against very few, if any, good things. In other words, you may be sixty to seventy-two compliments behind schedule. Ain't no bank in the world gonna lend you money with that payback record.

In this kind of situation, darn-right no one wants to listen to you. Me neither!

If you want to start being a leader, you have a lot of building up to do. You need to get in sixty or seventy-two—plus six—compliments before you will be in position to offer anyone some constructive criticism to help the team.

If this sounds like too much to you, then it's no surprise that you are not the leader you would like to be. Leadership requires a great deal of positive feedback, encouragement, and promotion before you can expect your corrections or criticisms to be successful.

Most athletes, after hearing a requirement like this, shake their heads and get a blank look on their faces. They don't associate eighty compliments with the phrase they've heard over and over: *You have to be willing to pay the price.*

Leaders see paying the price as a requirement for hard work, but not as a requirement to praise people they don't like. They thought they knew the price of leadership, but it turns out, they weren't even in the ballpark.

How do you praise someone who is messing up?

Easy. You overlook the stuff they are messing up on, and you compliment only the good things you see. Sometimes you have to look hard, and sometimes it's painful to overlook the things that need correcting. But that's *your* problem. If you want to be a leader, that's how it works. If you want to get people to start listening to you, you have to start saying things they like to hear. You're not being dishonest, just commenting frequently on the things that are good. When you make up for that past deficit plus six—when you have sat at home with a pen and a pad in your hand and the TV off and figured out ways to put new, fresh, realistic, and sincere compliments out there on the pile—you will be in position to make a suggestion or correction, and the objection about inattentive teammates will no longer be appropriate.

"I would like to lead, Coach," you say, "but my teammates don't want to hear what I have to say. They won't listen to me."

Yes they will. People like listening to people who say good things to them 85 percent of the time. People like listening to people who have thought up better ways to give compliments. It is very simple. Most athletes just don't want to work that hard. They aren't as willing as they think to pay the price because they don't understand the cost.

Leadership Energy

On purpose, I have run these two words together to make sure you understand what I hope to convey here.

What are the crucial ingredients required of a great leader? In none of the conversations, books, or programs about leadership that I am familiar with was adequate attention paid to the energy required of a true leader.

I imagine people sitting around a conference table or in an auditorium, at a seminar or in a class, discussing leadership.

Immediately, I picture folks jotting down notes, somebody yawning, and others rubbing their eyes or looking at their watches. I can't help but think that all of us interested in leadership probably ought to start with energy. You have to have a tremendous amount of energy to be an effective leader. Because, when all is said and done, when all of the "great leadership principles" are expounded and elucidated and explicated, you will probably find that most of the truly special exemplars of leadership—George Washington, Abraham Lincoln, Winston Churchill, Mao Zedong, Moses, this and that general—probably had more energy than those around them, and in most cases, they just outlasted their opponents. They did more, they talked more, they influenced more people. They were more active. A leader has to be incredibly active.

Line up today's leader wannabes, and you might do better putting your money on the Energizer Bunny. He keeps going and going . . .

In my realm, teaching point guards, if I were asked to name the one ingredient most lacking in the athletes with whom I work, it would be energy. Most of them, even though they truly aspire to be leaders, don't have the energy (or don't realize they have it) to do what I tell them needs to get done. In fact, they can't imagine that I truly mean what I say when I teach them to tell the center down the court—every time—to see the ball coming back on defense; to remind the shooting guard forty times per game to follow through; to urge aggressive block-outs on the free-throw line on every foul shot; to call out "Ball!" on every rebound; to warn of danger once or twice or three times on every defensive play; to use their teammates' names hundreds of times throughout a game; to fill the air in practice with—literally—a thousand reminders; to make sure the gym is constantly noisy; to respond to every negative with six positives; to encourage every player over and over again; to remind all their teammates every day of their strengths; and to keep the bench players excited and involved in every practice . . .

The list, throughout a week of teaching, gets longer and longer, and often the athletes get quieter and quieter. "I had no idea there was that much to it," they often say. But what they really had was no idea how much energy it would take to do over and over again what is quite easy to do once in awhile.

Energy. LeadershipEnergy. It's a giant step beyond feeling good and being in shape and a willingness to run and move and play hard. Most people have no idea the energy it takes to add constant clapping and talking and thinking and reminding on top of running and moving and playing.

You might guess that a hyperactive person has a better chance of being a great leader, and I would have to admit this truth. A hyperactive player has a much better chance than a smarter, better player with a low energy level.

Fortunately, energy levels aren't set in stone. Like just about everything else, LeadershipEnergy takes practice. With practice, LeadershipEnergy does improve. An out-of-shape person will tire with just one sprint down a court whereas a trained athlete will go up and down again and again, sometimes effortlessly. The same is true with an out-of-shape energizer. You can't expect to read about a crucial ingredient of leadership and then just go out on a court or field and give it. You will have to train yourself and work to improve your ability to give leadership energy. The more you train yourself to use leadership energy, the more able you will be to give it.

In the beginning, you could simply count your efforts. Run around one day with a tape recorder strapped to your waist, or put a camcorder near a practice court so you can go through the tape after an hour and count exactly how many times you said something, reminded someone of something, filled the air with positives, and clapped your hands with spirit. You—and they—will be surprised how dramatically you can improve your output if you care enough to measure it.

A Name is a Spotlight

Athletes, by nature, like to be in the spotlight. Even lazy, un-motivated athletes will hustle when the cameras are rolling, when the game is on national TV, and when important people are watching. This is why it is so important for you, as a leader, to put your teammates constantly in the spotlight or draw attention to them.

Typically, people think of this as a post-game thing, mentioning the efforts of overlooked players and making sure that unsung heroes get some recognition too—not just the guy who hit the winning shot. But to be truly effective, you can't wait for the post-game. Recognition and drawing attention has to happen daily, often during practice.

The difference between "Run hard!" and "Jeff, run hard!" is significant. *Run hard* will most often fall in the category of mere chatter that Jeff doesn't even hear, especially if he's thinking about other things, bothered by a personal problem, tired, being criticized by a coach, or feeling pressure of any kind. But say Jeff first, and Jeff hears. Not just his name but the command or urging that follows.

The more you put your teammates in the spotlight, the more effort they are going to give and the better they are likely to perform.

240 Names

Using names is so important that I suggest you think about saying them 240 times. That may initially sound like a lot. But in two hours of practice, calling out names 240 times would require you to say a name just two times each minute (120 X 2).

"Hustle, Bill. Nice pass, Mike!"

How long does that take? A second? Two seconds at the most.

So now what will you do with the next fifty-eight seconds, take a vacation?

Using teammates' names along with encouragement, reminders, and warnings ought to be so natural to you that the idea of tossing off 240 names during a typical practice would be easy. It should be unthinkable that you wouldn't do that. Yet most athletes don't even come close.

How does 480 or 960 sound?

Anyone out there planning to toss out a thousand names during the next practice? That's the way to put your teammates in the spotlight and help them to improve.

95

Leading by Example is Leading Poorly

One of the biggest errors in sports leadership is the notion that leading by example is a good thing. Many parents over the years have talked to me about their sons and daughters, and often they say something like: "He's quiet by nature. Doesn't say a lot. But his teammates respect him. He leads by example."

They never like my response, but I've learned to give it immediately, almost without thinking, rather than conceal the strength of my feelings: "If your son leads only by example, then he leads poorly."

Example is a very tiny part of leadership. Of course it's important to set a good example. But in my leadership model, "a good example" covers just one of the six crucial ingredients.

The ingredients of good leadership follow, but I wanted to get this example out of the way before we got started because I know how many athletes and parents would be reading through a bunch of pages thinking, "That's all very nice, but Johnny leads by example."

I want to make it abundantly clear that leading by example is an idea that gets far too much credit.

SCHAPE-ing a Practice Drill

The first subject in championship performance that I teach any group I work with is the concept of "SCHAPE-ing" activities. Athletes who want to be special can not afford to let games, drills, or any kind of activity go on without SCHAPE-ing those things in order to make them better.

SCHAPE-ing an action means adding six ingredients to it, to make sure the action is worthwhile and helps you and your team improve. In my opinion, this isn't just some nice-sounding concept for a locker room wall; it is something that must be a part of every athlete's commitment to his team on a day-by-day, hour-by-hour, minute-by-minute basis.

I want athletes to be conscious of SCHAPE-ing every activity in every practice; and when they fail even once, they can expect to hear instant criticism. If you aren't actively trying to SCHAPE a drill, you aren't practicing to your potential, and you are wasting your time.

SCHAPE comes from six crucial ingredients.

- **Spirit**
- **Communication**
- **Hustle**
- **Approach**
- **Precision**
- **Enhancement**

Spirit

Spirit is noise. A successful team must practice in a noisy, spirited atmosphere; otherwise, the players won't work up to their potential, they won't inspire each other, they won't energize each other. Given the natural ebb and flow of anyone's personality, feelings, and energy, you can expect every individual to experience some down time or at least some not-exactly-at-your-best time during the course of a practice. But this is much less likely to happen in an atmosphere where special efforts are being made to uplift each other.

A quiet gym is a loser's gym.

This line makes sense. The top teams don't practice in silence. Their coaches won't allow it.

No doubt there are a variety of ways to uplift athletes. But not many of them can be accomplished in silence. It is important that every team member understand that it is his responsibility to contribute some noise to the practice atmosphere, and it only takes one leader to remind everyone, over and over again, of that responsibility.

For example: "John, c'mon. Make some noise. Get Jimmy going. Pick Jimmy up. C'mon, John. What d'ya say?"

Communication I: Talk Ain't Cheap

Every good basketball coach tells his or her team to talk on the court. Nearly every person in the world would agree to the statement that communication elevates human experience. Yet athletes and would-be leaders fail very often to take advantage of this incredible tool.

Let me make this clear: communication does elevate human experience and it does very definitely improve a team's performance in sports. The better a team communicates, the better it plays. It's that simple. Let's look at some concrete examples.

First, we have already talked about the indisputable value of reminders. If you remind someone to do something, he is a lot more likely to do it than if you leave things to chance. Remind a teammate not to let #21 shoot, and there is much less chance that #21 will get a shot off the next time down the court. Forget to remind the defender, and the chances increase. That's not rocket science. Reminders are very effective tools in sports. But let's go into more detail to make sure those reminders work.

Communication II: Good NITE

I use the word NITE as an acronym to remind athletes of four important ingredients in good communication:

- Names,
- Information,
- Tone of voice, and
- Eye contact.

Use a person's name and you get his attention immediately, you put him in the spotlight, or put him on the spot, magnify his responsibility and get him to pay more attention so he can do his best.

Give information. Don't just chatter, but say things that are pertinent to the action of the moment. Remind a nervous person to relax, but go a step further. Tell him how. "Breathe deeply. Let it out slowly. Close your eyes. Make a fist, clench it hard, let it go. Imagine a peaceful scene." Urge your teammates to concentrate, and go a step further with informative detail. "Hold your follow-through, keep your arm up, fingers down, roll the ball off your fingertips." In every phase of the game, in every sport, there is an abundance of information that can be communicated to help an athlete perform better.

Tone of voice is important because most people feel excessively criticized and under-praised. As a result, many athletes tune out or rebel against negative criticism. I think most of the negatives should come from the coach, and teammates should learn how to communicate with each other in a positive, encouraging tone of voice. A positive, encouraging tone is a lot easier to listen to, over and over again; and helpful communication is so valuable that any good athlete needs to care about making his communication welcome.

Eye contact is important in nearly all forms of communication. Can you imagine buying insurance or a car or a new suit from a salesperson who never looked you in the eye? Go to any sales school and you will learn the importance of good eye contact. Yet athletes rarely get much schooling in sales techniques or effective communication. This crucial, performance-enhancing area is often left entirely to chance, to the detriment of everyone concerned.

On the court and off the court, it makes sense to use names, to share useful information, to speak in a positive, encouraging tone, and to make eye contact with your teammates—NITE communication. Athletes are very likely to forget the importance of NITE in the aftermath of a turnover, a botched play, or a mix-up on defense.

They shouldn't.

Off-the-court communication requires these ingredients as well; but most athletes completely leave off-the-court communication to chance. Usually, athletes talk off the court to their best friends and fail to talk at all to the teammates they aren't so close to.

Many plays which work during a game seem instinctive but actually happen as a result of off-the-court preparation. The coach, during limited practice time, can do only so much. Good teams add to the coach's efforts with off-the-court enhancements (which we will get to later). The better you communicate on and off the court, the better your team will play.

Hustle

Hustle is a word on every good coach's lips—constantly—and probably in every book on sports. So, I don't want to belabor such a well-known subject. If a player or team hopes to approach excellence, hustle is an absolute prerequisite.

Where I find the problem, or perhaps the issue not talked about enough, is the lack of hustle in practice, where it really counts.

Nearly all athletes—even lazy, selfish ones—hustle in games. And most athletes, deep inside (even though most are intelligent enough not to reveal these ideas to their coach) believe that they can loaf in practice or relax in practice and then turn it on and push it up a notch for games. And guess what? They are right. They can.

There's just one giant problem with approaching sports that way, and these part-time hustlers never seem to realize it. You can push your level of hustle up a notch for games, but you won't push your performance level up a notch unless you learn to hustle in practice.

You will never convince any good coach that taking it easy in practice is okay, unless you have concluded that you are as good as you can possibly be; therefore, the only important thing for you to do is be rested for the game so that you have plenty of energy to expend.

Successful coaches rarely think their teams are as good as they could be. A few more minutes on a new out-of-bounds play, another hour executing screens and rolls, another week on a new offense, another month on extending the team's shooting range, another year on increased strength . . . the list goes on.

There are so many areas of any sport that can be improved dramatically via extra attention that you really can't expect your coach to think your relaxing in practice makes any sense at all. It almost goes without saying that any hope of functioning as a leader will be lost if you try to communicate and add spirit to your team's practices but then loaf on the court yourself.

The people enamored with the concept of leading by example are correct in their belief that everything begins with hustle, with a good personal example. A leader does need an obvious commitment to spending effort every day in practice for everyone to see. You have to set a standard in this regard. You need to go from place to place on the practice court—in a hurry, always—as though maximizing time matters. (It does!)

Remember, you need to dive on loose balls and show the world a sense of urgency on defense, whether you are trying to stop the opposing team in the league championship or trying to stop your junior varsity during a Saturday morning scrimmage. Turning hustle off and on sets a lousy example, and it guarantees that your (and your team's) improvement will be very limited.

Approach

Your approach to the game of basketball or to whatever you do may seem initially self-explanatory. Some athletes are serious, some aren't. Your approach is either good or bad. That's what most athletes seem to think, and most athletes seem to think they have a pretty good approach to the game.

If you are an athlete and have read this far, you probably have a serious approach to the game. You really want to improve and you want to be considered a special player. That's why I have to give you this warning: a good coach finds almost every athlete's approach to the game inadequate, even the so-called dedicated athletes whose peers may call them coaches' pets.

To explain this clearly, let me give just one example from my Point Guard College program.

Before I can emphasize the meaning of the word *approach,* 99 percent of the athletes—during a scrimmage in which they are not involved—will pick up a ball and dribble it on the side of the court, toss a ball up to a side basket, turn their backs to the action and throw the ball against a wall!

I am going to repeat this for emphasis because the best kids do this routinely, unthinkingly, while the best coaches consider it absolute crap—an approach guaranteed to lead to team failure if you let it go on.

The best players, the most dedicated athletes in the nation, will turn their backs to a scrimmage and bounce a ball off a wall.

Some will bounce those balls very diligently, careful to aim the ball, roll the wrist, and follow through like a real shot. If an angry coach whizzed a ball one-eighth of an inch by their ear and shouted hotly, *What are you doing?* they would look at you like you lost your mind.

"Coach," the kid might answer, "since I wasn't involved in the action, I took a few moments to work on my shot-release and follow through."

I can picture a young, earnest, but inexperienced assistant coach quickly going to bat for the dedicated young man. "It's true, Coach. He wasn't messin' around. He was truly working on his shot, maximizing his time while waiting to get back in."

It sounds reasonable enough, but the experienced coach would then want to smack his *assistant* in the ear, not the player.

Maximizing his time, my butt!

On a basketball court, when your team is practicing, you don't maximize *your* time, you maximize the *team's* time. You keep your eyes glued to the action and demonstrate that you understand the Intelligent Observation-Commentary principle. Don't ever let yourself be fooled. There is no way you can have the same impact dribbling or shooting for a few isolated moments here and there as you can have being an intelligent observer-commentator.

Failing to understand this important principle is failing to lead a team. Period.

Intelligent Observation-Commentary

The best way I know to explain this principle is to ask you to imagine that Michael Jordan was standing on the side of the court during a game in which you were playing.

Will you for a moment imagine, too, the difference between Michael shooting off to the side and working diligently on his own game versus Michael watching your game and noticing some little things you are doing to help your team in a special way?

The difference in the meaning of the game and the meaning of Michael Jordan's presence on the court for you would be the difference between night and day.

It doesn't take a Michael Jordan to make a difference. Anyone can have an impact. The more astute the observer, the more meaningful the difference.

Since I don't guess any but the most dedicated athletes and coaches—astute observer-commentators—will bother reading a book like this, I can make this point even clearer: *your* careful observations and comments can mean a great deal to the participants in any game you ever have the opportunity to watch (assuming you are close enough to the action to offer instant commentary and reinforcement for little things that are rarely noticed and complimented).

Here is one example you will understand immediately.

Most basketball players have never heard of the concept of skirmishing. Some may occasionally do it but not be aware of it. Skirmishing is a defense technique: bluffing and faking a big movement or gesture to make an offensive player think you are going to do something you have no intention of doing.

Say you see a star player on the opposing team come dribbling down the court against one of your teammates, and you see him begin to come in your direction. The moment he looks in your direction, you make a big show as though you are going to charge out and double-team him. If you do it well enough, he may pick up his dribble, fumble his dribble, or maybe just turn and go the other way because your direction appears difficult. You look too ready, too animated for him to challenge you. Better to take the ball the other way where someone may be less alert and active.

The reason most players don't actively seek opportunities to skirmish, and thereby prevent opposing teams from doing the things they want to do, is that skirmishes are hardly ever noticed and complimented. Skirmishing helps teams, but most defenders never bother to skirmish.

Is the point becoming clear? Imagine what would happen if you saw a teammate in practice do a skirmish which discouraged a penetration, and you yelled out on the spot, "Nice ploy; that's great defense. Good help, Loida!"

Do you think Loida would be likely to stop more penetrations in the future with that same alertness and movement? Of course.

The problem is that Loida—if he ever tried a skirmish—never got a compliment, not even from a coach, and now he never does them anymore.

That is exactly what happens to most teams and most individuals. Because the team's approach to the game is so inadequate, the crucial "little things" that win games just don't get done, don't get complimented, and don't get repeated.

A lot of athletes say, "My coach is always talking about doing the little things. But he never says what they are. What are the little things? Is there a list of little things somewhere?"

My answer to athletes is probably equally frustrating: "I could make you a list, but it wouldn't do any good unless you had the right approach. You could memorize the list, but there would still be all sorts of other things that would come up and cause a loss, and we would still be forced to say that we hadn't done the little things again."

The little things become obvious and begin to get done more and more when your team's approach becomes excellent.

How do you spell approach? I-O-C. Intelligent Observation-Commentary.

I never allow my players to dribble or shoot or do anything on the side of a court except observe and comment. This works wonders for a team, but very few teams make a point of doing this consistently. Very few teams win championships, either.

Precision: Things Get Worse

The famous Second Law of Thermodynamics tells scientists (and any students that pay attention to their first year Physics or Earth Science classes) that things tend toward disorganization. People die, mountains crumble, and planets fly apart. So maybe it's not surprising that this principle crosses over so naturally into sports.

When a coach first shows a new drill, hoping this year's team will set dynamic screens, block out for rebounds every time, or run precise fast breaks, most athletes will concentrate on the drill on the first day. Once they understand the concepts being taught, they are likely to perform reasonably well. Unfortunately, with added practice, most drills get worse instead of better. Athletes quit concentrating; quit trying as hard; quit doing as well, unless they have a very active and demanding coach or—even better, a very active, demanding captain or leader who tries to improve performance each day, in each drill.

Probably fewer than one in a thousand athletes makes a serious attempt to get his or her teammates to strive for improvement each day in practice. It isn't easy. Athletes fall victim to that Second Law. They let their performance fall off. They are lazy by nature. Maybe everyone is. But this is something you have to fight, daily, if you plan to be a real leader who takes his team to a higher level.

You have to remind yourself every day, in every drill, that if you don't make a very active effort to enforce concentration and get your teammates to strive for precision, they will quickly slack off and enable more talented competitors or more dedicated "practicers" to beat you.

The only way I know to consistently beat more talented competitors is to practice more diligently so, when you meet in a game, your execution is clearly superior. (The only way to have superior execution at game time is to overcome the temptation to slack off and get through practices while looking forward to those games.) Practice time must be filled with consistent mental and physical effort to improve. This isn't easy, but there is one very comforting aspect of this whole subject.

Most athletes practice their sports so inefficiently that abundant opportunities for success exist for those who make the commitment to do sports right; who are willing each day to fight the Second Law; and who help their teammates by making sure fast-break drills, block-out techniques, offensive plays, and bench players get better each day in practice, instead of worse and worse.

Enhancement

It doesn't make much sense to talk about improving something until you have first made it right, adequate, or at least covered the basics. That's why, when talking about SCHAPE-ing a drill or a game or an activity on the court, you first have to talk about adding spirit, communication, hustle, approach, and precision to it. Then you can talk about enhancing it, making it even better.

If you are doing something silently, haphazardly, or slowly, there's no reason to look any further for improvement. You have to get those things in line first.

This is probably the reason few coaches ever talk to their players about enhancements. They never adequately get through the basics and, therefore, most athletes don't.

But if you are trying to be special, sincerely trying to win a championship, spending time off the court thinking about improving and winning and getting to another level of performance, then you have to think constantly about, not just meeting requirements, but how you can do things even better.

It's not hard to imagine how much better a team could become—and how much more fun their practices could be—if each player constantly thought about how he or she could make each on-the-court activity better.

One suggestion I have is this: try to make a game out of everything you do on the court. You don't need any set-up time, nor permission from a coach, nor a team meeting to do this. You just need your voice and, sometimes, a little creativity.

If you are in a small group working on a shooting drill, all you need to do is yell out, "Let's hit seven in a row!" and start counting and encouraging and urging along the way. It won't be hard to involve your teammates. Just about everyone tries harder and performs better when his performance is challenged and measured in some way. A shooter who might normally "just throw the ball up there" is much more likely to concentrate and try harder if you have announced that the group has five in a row and the next one, if he hits it, will be number six.

This scorekeeping won't change every player on your team instantly or turn everyone into 100 percent performers every time, but it certainly will help.

You can do this same thing even if you and your teammates are just working on a block-out drill or other technique that doesn't lend itself so easily to keeping score. Give style points the way judges do in the Olympics for diving and gymnastics.

Who's qualified to judge? *You!* Just do it. Start calling out numbers.

"Good pivot, good contact . . . That's a 6.9! . . . Good, keep up the good work! . . . Try to get a little lower and wider . . . That was almost a 7!"

It doesn't really matter what you say. The important thing is that you are involving your teammates in the activity and creating a sense of importance about what they are doing.

Keeping score isn't the only way to enhance an activity. Sometimes, enhancing an activity may require you to mop the court first (yes, I know that's not part of your job description), bring bandannas to practice, offer a crazy reward of some kind ("Winner gets an old hockey puck!"), or create some other kind of challenge or stimulation.

The specific things you start with, or even end up doing, are not nearly as important as this question: How often and how consistently can you bring this quality of mind to practice? How often can you just be there wanting and trying to make things better and getting your teammates to share your feelings?

Players and teams that are constantly trying to enhance what they are doing will definitely succeed.

Why Excuses Are So Bad

In every one of my books, I have written something very negative about excuses because they are so prevalent and so in need of alteration. Excuses hurt teams, not just because they waste time and kill team morale (and a coach's morale), but because they reveal that the player making them has a very off-line focus. An excuse-maker can't possibly be using his energy thinking about how to enhance what is going on or about to go on because, obviously, he is putting his time into explanations and justifications.

Maybe, in this context, you can better understand why a good coach hates excuses so much. When a player makes an excuse, especially on the court, it's hard for his coach to even think about the excuse itself. He gets a frown on his face before he even begins to hear the explanation. He frowns for the misplaced energy, not the reasoning.

This point ought to be compelling. If you truly wish to be a special athlete on a special team, you don't have time for excuses. You need all the time you can possibly muster to focus on things that will keep enhancing your team's activities in new and exciting ways.

Bowling Pins

One of the fortunate aspects of leadership is that moving even a large group of people is not nearly as difficult as it may seem initially. In fact it may be easy. However, most people's perceptions are so far off that they are apt to fail at bringing about some change because they don't consider the weakness of a group's resistance.

Unruly, lazy, or selfish people seldom have any cohesion or organization. They do not get together as a group, plan their behaviors, and work together. They are individuals going along with a crowd, easily influenced because they are without an agenda and lacking all but circumstantial support. In the midst of any group behavior, there are likely to be many people—even those most guilty—who are uncomfortable or don't fully agree with what is going on. They simply need to be mobilized in a different direction.

There is a scientific name for this phenomenon. It's called a phase transition.

Look at a school of fish. Many thousands swim in one direction, and you get the impression that there's a great determination at work, a force pulling the finned throng in the same direction. All of a sudden, usually for no apparent reason, the lead fish takes a sudden turn and the throng follows. Their new direction is as arbitrary as the first and just as unpredictable.

The simple fact is: group behavior isn't that hard to change. A person—a leader—simply has to be willing to make an effort. Change one person and then another, and suddenly a whole group can change. Many in the group may be uncomfortable with the mounting noise, hysteria, or whatever, and may be waiting anxiously and eagerly for someone to take charge and change things.

"But I didn't do anything" is never a valid excuse when things go wrong. A leader has to be willing to take a stand, to make clear what he or she believes is best. Leadership doesn't always work, but failing to try is *always* ill-advised, and failing to recognize the potential of one voice and of phase transitions can be crippling.

It is usually not one against many that you face in these kinds of situations. It is, instead, one against many *ones* with widely varying commitments to the current behavior. The secret, then, is to treat them all like the bowling pins they are. Just knock one down, and another and another, and pretty soon there is a decent chance they'll start knocking down each other without any additional effort from you. Suddenly, you're in a majority; your battles are two-on-one at every turn. The unorganized group members fall easily because they are now in a minority.

The first ones to sway are your friends, then your acquaintances and those who are smaller and weaker and younger than you. It doesn't take long to form a new group, one that stands in total and forceful opposition to the original unorganized group. Let seven people go to one of those unorganized individuals and watch the result. That's ganging up!

There is *no* excuse for failing to act. Most of the time, taking action is not merely noble, it works! Bowling pins just aren't that hard to knock over. Aim for the middle and throw yourself hard into it. The only failure is the failure to try. That's a real gutter ball.

"My team is lazy. My teammates are selfish."

I've had the opportunity several times in my life to work with losing basketball teams, and there's a thread of commonality among nearly all of them. Talk to the players individually and ask them what's wrong and you get just about the same answer over and over:

"I would like to play on a team with a group of players working together, sharing the ball and the limelight, but these guys . . ."

Go to the next guy.

"I would like to play on a team with a group of players working together, sharing the ball and the limelight, but these guys . . ."

Go to the next guy.

But need I continue? Each one is likely to tell you that he wants to do the right thing, that he has tried many times, but with this group it's hopeless. If only they all had different coaches and different teammates who wanted to do the right things, everything would be better and different. If only, if only.

After a while, what seems like an impossible task—working with all these selfish athletes—becomes daunting. They all want to be on a different kind of team and they all think they have done everything possible to change their team. But nothing has worked, so they've given up. They then join in the very actions they dislike, though in their minds, it's not because they want to. What choice do they have?

What choice do they have but to be selfish like everyone else? This kind of thinking is so obviously skewed, it requires no explanation. But it's incredible how often people think and justify their actions in those terms.

The only thing I can say is, I'm amazed at how quickly athletes, parents, and people in general seem to conclude that things are as they are and there's no use trying any longer to change them, even though many of their situations are extremely changeable.

When you find yourself in a situation that needs changing, get to work and change it. Start by doing one thing. Knock over one pin and then go on to the next. You will often be surprised at how easy it is.

Focus on One Influential Person

Here is a crucial point of good leadership that most athletes don't consider. It doesn't make sense to have some great ideas if no one will follow your suggestions. How do you get teammates or colleagues or associates to follow your suggestions? You don't! You get them to follow the suggestions of someone who they are already accustomed to following.

When you think of it this way, it makes perfect sense to almost everyone. But few of the athletes with whom I have ever worked seemed to do this consciously before we talked about it.

Take for example rhythmic clapping. On a basketball court, in order to liven up the gym and get athletes' minds off aches and pains and blisters and coaches' criticisms, it helps if a team will break out periodically into rhythmic clapping. (Chimpanzees have demonstrated that all sorts of clap combinations can be followed easily, so a group of athletes has no excuse.) This helps a team create a better atmosphere on the practice floor. When I coach, I require my players to do rhythmic clapping in practice, and I punish them when they fail to use this worthwhile tool.

But how does an athlete go from my program (where we use the technique often) to his or her own team and make it happen? What if a young sophomore is standing in a group of older players during a lull in practice and suddenly blurts out, "Hey, let's all clap and add some spirit to this atmosphere."

Clap-clap, clap-clap-clap. Clap-clap, clap-clap-clap. Clap-clap.

Works like a charm, right? Wrong. Chances are they all will look at him like he's an alien. "Where'd you learn *that*, cheerleading camp?"

They are likely to get a chuckle out of that question, and the sophomore will probably have been sufficiently chastised to keep him from making another suggestion all week.

Imagine the difference if the strongest or best player or the most experienced senior had suddenly said to the group, "We need to create some spirit in this gym. Let's start clapping and start making this atmosphere more positive."

When a physically strong player or a very talented (particularly older) player makes a suggestion like that, it's more of a demand, and it isn't very likely to be "chuckled off." The younger, less important players, especially if looked in the eye, are likely to join in the clapping immediately.

It doesn't make sense for a young sophomore to throw out the idea among older, better players and just hope for luck. It would be much more effective to talk to the star, the old guy, the one player who already has everyone's respect, and *get him to make the suggestion*. Convince him, off the court, and take time to explain the value of the clapping.

How do you get him, or that one special player, to listen to you? The answer is easy. However you can; whatever it takes.

When I was in college, the biggest player on my team could be "bribed" with Hostess Twinkies! If you asked him to stay after practice to work on a play or technique, he was likely to tell you he'd like to, but he had too much homework. I knew it was an excuse and I got past it quickly with the offer of a couple of packs of Twinkies. "Stay an extra fifteen minutes and I'll buy you two packs of Twinkies."

"Deal!" he said.

You just have to take the time to find out what will work. Does your star player need a date? Then you better start a black book of willing guinea pigs. No offense to anyone! I just mean that a true leader has to be versatile. You can't say, I don't have any money for buying extra Twinkies, and I don't even know any girls to date myself, so how can I get my big-ugly-illiterate center a date? That's just not the can-do attitude it takes to be a leader. A leader has to be not just resourceful, but proud of being resourceful. Being resourceful is a prime ingredient in the leadership recipe.

To be a good leader, you may very well have to mow some lawns or wash some cars to get extra money for other purposes. (Yes, money talks even in amateur sports!) And you probably will have to get over your social shyness in order to make the right things happen. The "black book" concept isn't as far-fetched as you may imagine either. It works!

In general, you have to take the time to find out what moves people—especially your team's most influential players or your company's most influential employees—and then you have to make those things available. "Everyone has a price" goes the old saying, and to a large extent it's true. You just have to be willing and able to find out what that price is. It's not always money, of course. But there's always something; you need to find it, and deliver it.

Harvey Mackay, a very successful businessman and author of *Swim with the Sharks Without Being Eaten Alive: Outsell, Outmanage, Outmotivate, and Outnegotiate Your Competition* and other books, counts a unique personal information sheet as one of the prime ingredients in the success of his company. Mackay's salespeople have to unostentatiously ask clients and potential clients eighty-five questions before his people can expect to succeed in making sales to those clients. That's a lot of questions. When you know eighty-five things about anyone, you know a lot. You know how to get that person to do all sorts of things because you know what he likes, what he dislikes, how he thinks, and what makes him tick.

So, back to the little sophomore with the big idea . . . He wanted to be a leader by tossing out a terrific suggestion in the middle of practice among the older players on his team, and all he got were quips and chuckles and put in his place.

He wanted to be a leader without paying the price of leadership, which means putting in the time to be in the position of leading effectively. In this case, that meant spending enough time with the best or toughest player on the team and making sure the good suggestion was presented in a way that would get it done.

As has often been said in other spheres, we live in a time when people have learned to expect or at least hope for instant gratification. Change the channel, flip the switch, go to Yahoo!, or pull in the drive-through. Get it *now*. Everyone, clap!

Nice concept when it works, but if you're going to be a leader, you can't expect instant responses, even to great suggestions. As the center on my college basketball team always said, "You gotta do your homework!"

You gotta put in time, be creative, and be resourceful. Leadership is not making a good suggestion that you learn at a leadership class and then basking in the joy of a grateful group of happy followers. It's rolling up your sleeves, getting down and dirty, getting immersed in the sludge, and then making the right things happen.

When you're young, inexperienced, or unaccustomed to leading or being followed, it makes sense to lead mostly through someone else. Lead the leader, influence the influencers. Just know in advance that the key to your leadership is not knowing what to suggest to the group, but rather taking the time to get to know the person who already knows how to move the group.

Moving a Teammate

One of the most important and overlooked skills of a good leader on the court (usually the point guard's job), is to be able to move a teammate quickly in order to make a play or to make a play more likely to succeed. All sorts of inexperienced players will claim they can do this, but usually, if they do it at all, they do it at the wrong times and in the wrong way.

First, you move a teammate like a friend, not like an angry boss. In other words, instead of gesturing and pointing and yelling impatiently—after that, it's usually too late—you need to recognize spacing problems and opportunities quickly; and you usually need to discuss those situations in advance so when they arise, a quick glance and a nod will be all that are necessary to create the action you want. And it's hardly ever noticeable to the average fan.

There are, of course, times when a more emphatic voice

or gesture may be necessary, but more often leadership is a matter of timing and planning and reminding, not of yelling and impatiently criticizing.

The problem with so many players who consider themselves good ball handlers (they are usually only good dribblers) is that they aren't as aware as they should be of how important good spacing is to the successful running of a play. As a result, they seldom think about the value of moving a player to create an opening. They can hit the open man perhaps, but they rarely see opportunities to get a man open, or to create openings.

A good leader on the court should try to become aware of the times, for example, when two teammates are standing close together, allowing just one defender to cover them both and permitting another defender to double-team or to get away with loafing. At times like this, a bit of patience may produce big dividends. Hold the ball, look one of your teammates in the eye, call out his name and make a motion, either with your hand or eyes or both, where you want him to go. If you're asking him to go where he's rarely gone before, he's not likely to follow your lead in time to make the play successful. But if this is a situation that arises often (perhaps at the end of one of your plays), during or following practice you should be able to talk about where would be best for him to go. After a discussion like this, usually all you need to do in the game is make direct eye contact with him at the moment he should be moving. A sudden, direct stare can be as effective as the blast of a starter pistol.

Inexperienced leaders are more inclined to be on the court barking and gesturing like frantic traffic cops, whereas experienced leaders will get a lot more done with nods and looks and maybe the inaudible call of a teammate's name at the moment of eye contact. Most fans will fail to notice any of this leadership, and most players just don't understand.

How often do you move a teammate into a better position in order to make a play? You don't want to be the kind of player who is so busy dribbling and seeking a shot that you fail to see the possibilities around you. Often, big openings are just a slight movement or a small adjustment away.

Team Leadership

Leadership does not mean one player barking out commands and the rest of the team waiting to carry them out. A true leader empowers everyone else to lead so that leadership is shared and spread among all members of the team.

No player should wait to be called upon or to be elected captain. It is possible and necessary for you and every team member to take on leadership responsibilities as soon as you are able.

How do you do that? By doing what a good leader does: reminding, encouraging, communicating, hustling, and so on.

If you are the captain, focus your attention on getting everyone to do the things that need to get done. If you are not the captain, consider focusing your attention on the captain and on trying to reinforce his leadership. If he is quiet or reluctant to lead, you still have to do the things that are necessary (to help your team maximize its potential), and you probably should spend a lot of time helping the captain to do those things too.

Instead of taking over for a quiet captain, you can subtly emphasize the things he has said and encourage your teammates to do those things. This will reduce ill feeling and enable you to continue to lead without drawing the same degree of resentment you might get otherwise if you bypassed your captain.

All leadership, at any level, must take into consideration the desires, egos, and personal situations of individuals; therefore, it should be obvious that you don't want to treat a quiet captain as though he doesn't exist. Instead, resort to the 6-to-1 ratio, talk with him off the court, and make sure you know what he wants. With proper respect paid to him and his position, you will be able to do all the things that need to be done without having any title at all. He will probably appreciate your support.

When a good leader has pushed and pulled and prodded and pleaded and finally done his work well, the men he has led so well are apt to say, "We did it ourselves."

I don't recall who originally explained leadership that way, but I've always thought it was wise. It offers a blueprint for how to lead successfully, whether as the team captain or one of many team members. If you lead really well, it shouldn't be too obvious to anyone. The people around you should be too busy doing their jobs and fielding the compliments you are spreading around and getting others to spread.

The time is always right to do right. Consider yourself always in position to lead.

Talking Trash: The ETDMTYS Approach

Trash talking is a big subject in sports, but I never pay any attention to it. In my opinion, a good leader doesn't have time for it. There are so many better things you can do with your time.

The purpose of this section isn't about trash talking in that sense. It is about real trash, though picking up trash is only a very tiny part of what I call the *Expect To Do More Than Your Share* approach to sports and life. (I pronounce it "Et-D-Mitas.")

The ETDMTYS approach is not most athletes' or most people's way of doing things, but it is the way of a leader: expecting routinely to do more than your share. More than your share of hustling, more than your share of encouraging, more than your share of praising, more than your share of work to help the team win.

More familiar is the approach that asks *Why do I have to do that? He didn't have to do that?* Or *Why do I have to pick up that trash? I didn't throw it down.*

A leader or anyone who wants to inhabit a special environment has to expect to do extra in order to create that special environment. I like the analogy of land. Consider for a moment the difference between a country club golf course, like the one where the Masters is played in Augusta, Georgia, and a neglected lot.

Two hundred years ago there may have been almost no difference in those two plots of land. But over time, things happened. The one plot was turned into a showplace golf course with groundskeepers and caretakers and maintenance crews, while the other became a dumping ground. The two plots of land are essentially the same, but the respect that people now have for them is very different. Now people who regularly dump all sorts of junk on the vacant lot wouldn't think of throwing even a tiny gum wrapper on the course at Augusta.

What happened?

The one piece of land was valued and cared for. The other wasn't. It was allowed to get worse and worse.

There is a tendency to think of people who litter as being bad and people who don't as being good. But what turns out to be more often true is that most people have both potentials. We tend to litter land that seems unrespected, and we are careful and respectful of land that is valued. In other words, the value placed on something by people is the prime motivator of other people.

This fact should bring into focus why picking up trash in general and expecting to do more than your share routinely is so important to a leader. Do you want to live in a place where people don't litter? You better plan on picking up a lot of extra litter until the majority of people sense that this place is valued, and therefore they should treat it accordingly.

But won't some jerks still litter? Of course. The work of a leader is never finished. But leadership, as well as cleanup, becomes a lot easier as more and more people go along with the trends.

I hope you have already caught the point for sports. Do you want to play for a respected coach? Then respect the coach and get your teammates to do the same—even if your coach hasn't learned yet to demand respect.

Do you want to play on a team that hustles? Then you better plan on hustling extra, setting a terrific example, and working hard on your teammates to get them to hustle.

Do you want to play on a team that is unselfish? Then plan on being extremely unselfish until the rest of your teammates start to get the idea.

Don't let yourself fall into the trap of thinking, "I would like to do this or that, but they won't."

People won't quit tossing trash on the lot till someone works extra hard and cleans it up, talks to others and keeps on working, and then finally breaks the others' habits and alters the cycle of disrespect.

ETDMTYS. Expect to do more than your share. People who want to play on a special team, live in a special neighborhood, and have pride in a special country must have this approach.

Some people experiment occasionally with doing a little extra here and there, but they soon get discouraged with others' lack of cooperation. I think a good leader has to assume that others will be very slow to cooperate and do what is necessary, while not looking constantly over his or her shoulder for reinforcement. They must simply do it because it is the way to get good things accomplished and the way to go through sports and life feeling proud.

Expect to do more than your share on the court and off. It really isn't hard once you get accustomed to it.

Leadership in Action

Matt Dyment was a basketball player at Linfield College in McMinnville, Oregon. He is also one of the finest leaders I have ever seen on and off a basketball court. I offer some examples of Matt's leadership as a yardstick so you can measure your own efforts by comparison.

The off-season letter. This is an ideal way to begin a season, to lay out a goal and a commitment to your coach and your teammates. Here is the letter that Dyment sent to his coach, with the request that his coach send a copy to each of the members of the team.

To the Future Linfield National Champions Hoops Team,

> "He is no fool who gives what he cannot keep to gain what he cannot lose."
>
> —Jim Elliot

119

I hope that your two months of vacation time have been the best ever. As for me, I have been working my tail off looking forward to our upcoming season. Six days ago, Aaron Lee and I began lifting and shooting for (around) two hours a day. (My position of head toilet cleaner on campus has given me the wonderful privilege of gym key use.)

Summer for all of you should now be over. It's time to begin paying the price for a National Championship, for which the cost is not a small one. We need to be putting more time in than any other team in the nation. We have the talent, we have the character; all we have to do is now pay the price in the weight room, on the court, and in our minds.

"Anything the mind can conceive and believe, it can achieve."

—Larry Southers

Do you believe that we can win the NC baby? What are you doing to match your beliefs? If you truly believe that we can win the National Championship, your life will be changed. Work out at top speed, push yourself beyond anything you have ever known, and dream of the days to come.

The only thing that we lack to this point right now is playing together and knowing each other, which is a big ingredient to being a championship caliber team. In order to offset this problem, we are going to have to be very exclusive with our play. To win big, we must sacrifice big. I have gone ahead and made some preliminary plans for the fall, and I would like to bounce them off you guys as soon as the school year starts.

The Varsity team will be meeting at Coach Doty's house the first three days of school—Wednesday, Thursday, Friday—for BBQ's up there to go over our fall game plan and pre-training discussions. Begin putting time in now with extra running, shooting, and lifting so that we can get a phat jump on becoming the first National Championship team Linfield hoops has ever had.

God bless all you guys. I look forward to seeing you soon.

—Dy #23.

The following incidents I witnessed in a week of being around the Linfield team. Research was unnecessary, though I'm sure more examples of Matt Dyment's leadership would be obvious if I had decided to undertake it.

Team dinners. The team got together once per week for dinner at someone's house or apartment. Nothing fancy, just a chance to increase interaction off the court and for all the guys to get to know each other better in a relaxed environment. I'm not sure that Matt initiated the idea for these dinners, but I'd bet on it!

Lunchtime workouts—with camcorder. Usually Matt works one-on-one, aiming at increasing explosiveness off the dribble. Set up on a tripod, the camcorder gives Matt the opportunity to see, later in the day, just how much effort he puts out, how violently he fakes or explodes, how abruptly he stops, how well he follows through on his shots, and how disruptive his defense is.

Shooting schedule—with chart. Not just shooting around. "Game speed" he calls it, with a teammate. Each group of shots is counted and charted so he knows if he's improving each day or getting worse.

Team meetings. Called as needed. Sometimes to urge greater effort, sometimes to remind everyone of their commitment and what it will take to get there.

Team videos. Matt asks his coach if he can take home the filmed scrimmages, despite the fact that the team already sees clips of the plays the coach considers particularly important. I think he shows these videos to team members in addition to watching them alone. There is no question that Matt does more than "a little bit extra."

Practice warm-ups. Matt leads pre-practice and pre-game stretches each day and helps the team, with reminders, to get in a frame of mind to play to the best of their ability.

Practice startup. Before the coach arrives on the court to begin practice, Matt is always there early with the rest of his teammates, getting warmed up, running plays, and working on things that the team needs. He is truly a coach on the court. You get the feeling that, if the coach didn't show up, practice would go on as usual, productive without him.

Practicing with Aaron Lee. Matt does many of his extra workouts with a friend on the team. Their workouts and extra efforts have a contagious impact on other team members, even those who are not as ambitious, energetic, or committed. Plus, no one can be unaware of the 2-on-1 effect of being in opposition to these guys.

Informal meetings with the coach. Matt walks into his coach's office once or twice a day for a few minutes just to see what's going on, maybe to share one idea, or maybe to ask one question or make one suggestion. The coach can't possibly be unaffected by the obvious nature of Matt's full commitment.

Scouting with the coach—with camcorder. It was November 12, I think (still twelve days before the start of their season) when Matt decided, along with two teammates, to ride with his coach and watch the game of a future opponent. Matt brought a camcorder so he could tape the team's plays. (Turns out that's against NCAA Division III rules, so once informed during the game, Matt walked downstairs and handed the tape over to a school official.)

Response to innovation. During a team meeting with the coach, after a new substitution pattern had been explained, Matt made this comment: "I can think of 106 reasons why I don't like it, but I also understand coach's points and I think it does have a chance to help our team. So, I'm buying into it."

Communication on the court. In every practice, you hear Matt reminding his teammates to play hard and to do the things necessary to win a national championship. Often that reminder comes in the form of two letters: "NC, NC." Matt keeps the national championship in his mind constantly, and he makes an active effort to keep it in his teammates' minds during practice.

Hustle on the court. Strawberries on both thighs, knee pads on both legs. No one on Matt's team has a chance to doubt his commitment. Matt is not reluctant to get on the floor (to put it mildly).

In the weight room. First, Matt makes sure everyone remembers when it's a lifting day, then encourages and reminds during the lifting.

Understanding human behavior. Matt's coach says that Matt probably understands his teammates and his coach—and human behavior in general—better than any player he has ever coached. Matt is tuned into his teammates. He told his coach about one player's girlfriend problems (the kid got dumped!) and discussed some other players who didn't share his level of commitment.

Team conditioning. When lack of gym space, an extra-long film session one day, and other atypical events limited the team's on-the-court time for a few days, Matt put the team through an extra conditioning effort, reminding them when they thought they were finished, "One more. One more. NC, baby, NC."

A coach's dream. His coach feels more relaxed coaching this team than any other. Surprise? Hardly. With the team in the hands of Matt Dyment, any coach ought to be able to relax. Where does he find the time? Doesn't Matt Dyment have a life, go to class, have a girlfriend, read the paper, go to movies? From all indications, Matt has it all. A religious commitment too, plus a girlfriend named Carla and a graduation with honors ahead—in four years.

How does he do all that? Budgeting time, maximizing time? Of course. That goes without saying. From what I could observe and surmise, Matt puts a tremendous amount of time, thought, and energy into everything he does. He is serious about life and enjoys life too.

No doubt there is a lot more to know and say about Matt Dyment, but I think this is enough to give a clear idea of the way to approach sports and life in general. If this kind of commitment seems too much for "just a game," I think you need to find some other activities that inspire you to approach them with Matt's level of commitment. Clearly, this kind of commitment is the key to gaining the respect of peers and of people in general; it's the key to feeling personal happiness and fulfillment; and it's the key to success in whatever you do.

I have no idea if Linfield College will win a national championship. Sports, like life, takes unexpected twists and turns. But a leader like Matt Dyment sure gives a team a better chance.

Matt's friend, Aaron Lee, asked his coach for the class schedule of the team's 7-footer. Matt and Aaron were worried about the big guy remaining academically eligible, and they didn't want to wait around hoping he would pass everything. Their goals were team goals, and they knew a 7-footer sometimes helps a basketball team reach the promised land. They didn't want to take any chances, and they planned to check on him.

That's leadership.

Magic

Magic Johnson was perhaps the best point guard and one of the best leaders in the history of basketball. A superstar for the Los Angeles Lakers and a point guard at 6'9", Magic had a lot going for him, including a terrific personality and a way with people. These special qualities got him a national TV talk show—not exactly typical of ex-jocks—but they also helped him with the other thing for which he is well known. While still a superstar performer, Magic Johnson had to retire from basketball because he contracted the HIV-virus from one of his many girlfriends.

Whether you agree or disagree with Magic's lifestyle (he paid a high price for it), that lifestyle is instructive for any would-be leader. How a guy could go about keeping several girlfriends at the same time requires, strangely perhaps, very much the same "strategy," or methods, as a good point guard and leader needs to keep a group of teammates happy.

Since Magic Johnson was proficient at both having girlfriends and leading a team, it is worthwhile to examine Magic's strong points. To me, it all boils down to one simple fact: Magic was very good at making people feel special. When you make people feel special about themselves, they will like you and perform their best for you. It's simple and magic. I hope you can see how these two activities (making girlfriends and teammates feel special) require the same methods.

[The people at the Good Citizens Bureau will want me, like a good martial arts instructor, to make sure here that you promise to use these methods only for good—only to help a team win and not to keep four or five lovers on the line! Do you promise?]

Since you promised, I am going to deal first with how to keep four girlfriends (or boyfriends) feeling special, and you should be able to make the easy connections to your teammates on the basketball court.

If you want to keep four girlfriends at the same time and keep them all feeling special, you have to have a lot of energy. You have to give special time to all of them, private time to each one. You have to go out of your way, often, to call them, send them letters, stick post-it notes on their books, give them sincere compliments, encourage and support them, and to express your appreciation and confidence in them—privately.

There's a bit of a lie involved, I guess you could say, in that the compliments won't have the same force if they are expressed within hearing range of a whole group. ("Hey, y'all are really beautiful. We should get together sometime!") One at a time, whether with teammates or friends, your communication will have real impact (will be magical) when you give each one the feeling that you appreciate special things about him or her in special ways. ("Ah, you have the prettiest eyes.")

Naturally, the more tuned in you are to another person, the better chance your communication will reach him or her. A note complimenting a woman's beautiful red hair isn't going to go over very well if she is blond! Just like a compliment on your fine hook shot isn't going to turn you on if you never shoot a hook.

Complimenting someone's unique way of carrying himself or herself or a player's ability to draw fouls or catch a defense player napping can be very effective and much appreciated if the person being complimented feels you are sincere, that he or she deserves the praise and recognition, and is truly valued by you.

So, back to Magic Johnson. What made him so effective? With his special personality, expressive eyes, terrific laugh, and unique way, it wasn't difficult for him to make Kareem feel that his "sky hook" was unstoppable, or to make Byron Scott feel like his outside shot was "a sure three anytime," or to make James feel very Worthy indeed when he out rebounded and outran the NBA's less talented power forwards. In the same way, it isn't difficult to imagine the impact Magic was able to have on women when he gave them his full attention, looked them in the eyes, and told them they were beautiful and wonderful to be with. Magic brought out people's best. His attentions hit home.

Whether you use this advice to get extra "friends"—you scoundrel, you—or use Magic's methods to win basketball games is up to you. Just don't plan to win at anything without the crucial ingredients needed to make those around you feel special.

Tune in. Be enthusiastic. Compliment. Empower. Encourage. Invite. Include. Question. Stare. Thank. Express your feelings. Take time at unexpected moments to make sure they feel appreciated for their special talents.

At crunch time, a great point guard makes all four teammates feel his or her expectation that they have what it takes to succeed. They have their doubts—most everyone does— but they are buoyed by their leader's confidence in them. There ought to also be some players on the bench who have the feeling that you would like to see them get in the game because you have special confidence in *them*.

Communicate in special ways. Make your teammates—and coaches—feel special about themselves, and you will accumulate a lot of power. What happens from there is up to you. And Magic.

As a Person
A Personal Report Card

The Personal Report Card

Each year, before athletes come to my summer programs, they are asked to fill out personal information sheets so I can learn some things about them before they arrive. One of the questions is so consistently answered in the same and (for me) unexpected way, that it has had an impact on the way I think and has inspired this section of the book.

The statement on the sheet says: *Please evaluate yourself as a student, as a person, and as an athlete.*

The answers are amazingly consistent. Hundreds write that they are excellent students. How could they not be? Many of them get all A's; they have 4.3 (or more) grade point averages or advanced placement classes that provide college credit and are "weighted" beyond the value of an ordinary course; and they won a poetry contest or science fair or a spelling bee. They are excellent students. Everyone agrees.

Almost all of the respondents try to be modest but, clearly, they view themselves as excellent people. How can they not? They write that they have a lot of friends; they are respected in their schools and communities; they win citizenship and student-athlete awards; and, probably most important, they try to treat others the way they would like to be treated. Sounds like excellence, doesn't it? At first, anyway.

Finally, they get to the athlete part, and nearly everyone says "Fair" or "Okay." Beyond that they usually write a rather succinct explanation. Although they won this or that MVP or All-Conference award, they realize they are no Michael Jordan. They work hard, they usually say, but they know they have a lot of improving to do.

Do you get what has so often caught my eye? Three categories of human endeavor and, over and over again, the same three responses: Excellent student. Excellent person. Fair athlete.

In my opinion, they are correct on only the third evaluation where they have in mind the standard set by Michael Jordan.

But why are they so blind to the standards of excellence in those other, even larger areas? Are they not aware that American students are considered to be inferior to students all over the Western World? Why do our schools persist in letting so many young people think of themselves as excellent when there isn't anyone near an Einstein among them?

I'm not going to go off on a tirade about the American school system except to say that it seems clear to me that we are badly in need of a different standard of evaluation.

Every high school student ought to realize that Einstein or someone of that stature is the standard—that is, say, a 10—and their 4.0s and 4.3s indicate a level far below that top level, with plenty of room for improvement. Wouldn't that alone make tens of thousands of American students a lot more likely to raise their levels of achievement?

I think our school systems are totally missing the boat by failing to provide a higher standard of comparison. Working with students in all fifty states, I think I can say unequivocally that this is a national problem, a national failing that could be easily rectified. An "A" in a high school course should be seen for what it is: an indication of a certain standard of achievement for a very low level of expectation.

More importantly, I think, is the notion of excellence as a person on the part of young people who are, in fact, very average. For example, though they may win citizenship awards and think they try to treat others the way they would like to be treated, I would presume they fall far short of any standard of excellence that would arise should a group assemble to consider the elements of good citizenship or humanity.

Stemming from the need for a standard of personal excellence, I offer a citizenship test or "State of the Person" report card.

In brief, here are twenty-one categories or subjects in which I think each person should strive to get an A. In my opinion, all A's in these would qualify a person to think of himself as approaching excellence as a person in the same way Michael Jordan approached excellence as a basketball player.

How do you measure up?

State of the Person Self-Test Report Card

1.Concentration

Are you able to focus fully on whatever it is you are doing? If you can be left off in a library in a strange town and amuse yourself effortlessly for six or seven hours, this would be a step in the right direction. If you can pick up a book in any subject and study it for two consecutive hours, this would be another step. A good person ought to be able to concentrate.

2.Systematic Improvement

Do you consistently work on goals and measure daily performance levels so you can clearly chart your improvement? Without a plan and a method of periodic measurement, you really can't claim to be maximizing your talents. If you don't have a chart or two in your home that you mark daily, or at least twice a week, you surely are achieving below your capacity.

3.Curiosity

Are your classes exciting? Are ideas exciting? Are people interesting to you? Or do you chuckle at the idea of going to an opera, a ballet, or a lecture at the local university or library? Have you been to a gay rights meeting? A demonstration? A debate? Ever turn the TV on purpose to something you normally wouldn't watch just to enlarge your sphere of knowledge and awareness? It ought to be possible to get curious about any subject at all. If you ever claim to be bored, you aren't even halfway there on this one.

4.Cheerfulness/Enthusiasm

Do you seem happy to be alive at home and in school? Are

you consistently excited by people, school, and opportunities? And is it obvious to everyone? Are you a joy to be around because you add a spark and energy to life? The famous opera singer Beverly Sills, who had a lot of misfortune in her life, once said, "I may not ever be happy, but I hope I can always be cheerful."

5.Workmanship/Production

What can you show off? Paintings, pottery, papers, poems, notebooks? What is the look of the papers you turn in to teachers? Are you proud of the way you represent yourself? What do you have that is concrete and substantial to show for your time on this planet? If someone snooped around your things, what could they find that presents evidence of your good efforts?

6.Gratitude

Have you written a thank-you note recently? Do you write at least one per month? So many people do so much—parents, teachers, coaches, janitors, cooks—and rarely do they get any thanks for their good deeds and efforts. It would be impossible to ever thank parents enough. (How many diapers have *you* changed lately? It's not as fun as it looks!)

7.Work Ethic

Do you impress your parents, teachers, and coaches with how much energy and effort you put into the things you do? How often do people marvel at your capacity to work? How many teachers have told you that you are the hardest working student they have? How often has your coach told you that you are the hardest working athlete on the team? A special work ethic is universally admired.

8.Self-discipline

Are you consistent about taking personal responsibility for hygiene, waking up in the morning, going to bed at night, beginning to study, turning in homework assignments, having a regular study place, and establishing useful routines? A person with excellent self-discipline rarely has to be reminded to do anything but often reminds others.

9.Treatment of People

Do you treat your parents as people? How is your treatment of teachers and strangers? What are your comments to others? How many people do you uplift in a typical day? How many people feel empowered and more confident as a result of your support? Are you encouraging and supportive of friends and acquaintances?

10.Uplift

Do you make atmospheres better? In class, at home, in the gym, via trash, via talk? What impact do you have on your surroundings? Are the places you occupy improved as a result of your being in them?

11. Seriousness

Are you serious about the things you do and aware of the impact you can have on others and on your own future?

12.Communication

Do you understand that reading, writing, speaking, and listening skills are valued throughout the world? How is your eye contact, hand shaking, sentence structure, empathy, expression? Are you taking full advantage of the remarkable powers of sincere, effective communication?

13.Physical Fitness

Are you giving your body the opportunity to enhance your life via energy level, appearance, strength, sport? Do you maintain a regular regimen of fitness?

14.Moderation

Are you intelligent, in control, and aware of the consequences of your actions? Do you moderate your own urges as well as your own judgment of others' actions?

15.Generosity

Do you find ways to give away a lot of the things you have so that others can enjoy them? Do you need a lot of material things to be happy, or are you more interested in getting material things for others?

16.Thinking and Reasoning

How well do you deal with problems, evaluate opinions, and form your own ideas? What religions have you studied? What foreign or unusual ideas and philosophies have you weighed? Could you help Palestinians and Israelis, for example, to find some areas of common ground and help solve their problems?

17.Broadmindedness

How do you respond to other cultures and religions, unusual ideas, unexpected comments, and different tastes in fashion? Do you do anything to try to expand your tolerance and objectivity?

18.Desire to Meet Challenges

What energy and effort do you bring to subjects you don't like in school, activities that are new to you, problems that are difficult to solve, and conflicts in your home or among friends?

19.Toughness

How good are you at overcoming fatigue in school, during homework, and in sports? How good are you at taking criticism? How quick are you to complain or blame? How good are you at taking full responsibility for the circumstances that confront you? Do you control circumstances or do you let them control you?

20. Outreach

How often and how well do you reach out to include and invite others to show off their talents, express their feelings, and share your friends and interests? It would be difficult to be too good at this.

21. Self-Pride

What would you want the world to see if *60 Minutes* broadcasted a documentary report on you? Would you be a terrific role model to the rest of the world if they suddenly got an inside, detailed look at the way you live your life? Would you be proud of what the world would see?

All A's?

Is it hard to do all these things? You betcha. It's hard to bring the ball down the court against Gary Payton, contain Allen Iverson and slam dunk on Shaq too. But that's what Michael Jordan and excellence are all about in basketball. Should excellence as a person be any easier?

Index

ABOUT THE AUTHOR

Dick DeVenzio gave his life to sports and to a set of beliefs, ideas and convictions mostly related to the intelligent pursuit of excellence in sports. The son of a very successful basketball coach, Dick grew up wanting to be a basketball star. That led to daily schedules and all-day practicing by the time he was in 7th grade. By 10th grade, he was a varsity starter, averaging 20 points a game—at 5'-6", and the next year he averaged 30—at 5'-9". In his senior year, he led Ambridge High School to an undefeated state championship, and his team is still considered the best ever to play in Pennsylvania. His name is in the Basketball Hall of Fame, on Parade Magazine's 1967 All-American First Five.

Two years later, at Duke University, Dick was an All-ACC selection, and in 1971, a First Team Academic All-American.

After graduating from Duke, Dick played and coached professional basketball in Europe and South America and founded the now nationally acclaimed Point Guard College.

Considered by many to be a basketball genius and a gifted writer, Dick's writings and basketball programs have inspired and influenced countless coaches and athletes. He died in 2001 at age 52.

Other books by Dick DeVenzio:

STUFF Good Players Should Know:
  Intelligent Basketball from A to Z

Think Like a Champion:
  A Guide to Championship Performance for Student-Athletes

There's Only One Way to Win:
  Lessons from a Legend

To order books, go to www.pointguardcollege.com.